Reno v. ACLU:

internet censorship

SUPREME COURT MILESTONES
Reno v. ACLU:
Internet censorship

JOAN AXELROD-CONTRADA

Marshall Cavendish
Benchmark
New York

With special thanks to Professor David M. O'Brien of the Woodrow Wilson Department of Politics at the University of Virginia for reviewing the text of this book.

Marshall Cavendish Benchmark
99 White Plains Road
Tarrytown, NY 10591
www.marshallcavendish.us

Library of Congress Cataloging-in-Publication Data
Axelrod-Contrada, Joan.
Reno v. ACLU : Internet censorship / by Joan Axelrod-Contrada.
p. cm.— (Supreme Court milestones)
Includes bibliographical references and index.
ISBN-13: 978-0-7614-2144-3
ISBN-10: 0-7614-2144-0
1. United States—Trials, litigation, etc.—Juvenile literature. 2. American Civil Liberties Union—Trials, litigation, etc.—Juvenile literature. 3. Internet—Law and legislation—United States—Criminal provisions—Juvenile literature. 4. Obscenity (Law)—United States—Juvenile literature. 5. Freedom of speech—United States—Juvenile literature.
I. Title: Reno versus ACLU. II. Title. III. Series.
KF228.U5A96 2006
344.7305'31—dc22 2005029837

Photo Research by Candlepants Incorporated
Cover Photo: AP Wide World Photos

The photographs in this book are used by permission and through the courtesy of: *AP/Wide World Photos*: 1, 2–3, 28, 33, 35, 39, 58, 74, 81, 83, 105, 112; *Corbis*: Jason Reed/Reuters, 11, 98, 102; Bettmann,18; *Wildcat International/Photo by Greg Money*: 13; *Rheana Parrenas*: 14; *Photography Collection, Miriam and Ira D. Wallach Division of Art, Prints and Photographs, The New York Public Library, Astor, Lenox and Tilden Foundations*: 21; *Photo Courtesy Anthony Coppolino*: 49; *Office Courtesy of Hon. Dolores K. Sloviter*: 55; *Photo Courtesy Philadelphia Fight*: 61.

Series design by Sonia Chaghatzbanian

Cover caption: Ann Beeson, associate legal director of the ACLU, stands outside the Supreme Court, explaining why the ACLU does not support the 1998 Child Online Protection Act.

Printed in China

135642

CONTENTS

Introduction

SHOULD THE U.S. GOVERNMENT protect young people from "obscene" and "indecent" material on the Internet? That's the question that faced the U.S. Supreme Court in 1996 in the landmark case of *Reno* v. *ACLU*. The case pitted the U.S. government, represented by Attorney General Janet Reno, against a coalition of groups headed by the American Civil Liberties Union (ACLU).

Known as "the case to overturn the Communications Decency Act" (CDA), *Reno* v. *ACLU* involved an act of Congress signed into law by President Bill Clinton on February 8, 1996, that made it a crime to send "indecent" or "patently offensive" material over the Internet to anyone under the age of eighteen. The ACLU immediately filed suit to prevent the new law from taking effect while the case was being tried. A federal judge granted the ACLU's request in part, and then the ACLU got the government to voluntarily refrain from enforcing the rest of the law until the case was resolved in court.

Reno v. *ACLU* took place in the mid-1990s, but, in cybertime, it seemed like a different era. The Internet was just getting started. A new word—cyberporn—burst on the scene in a flurry of high-profile media stories. Senator J. James Exon, the Nebraska Democrat who sponsored the CDA, said that the raw images of cyberporn made *Playboy* and *Penthouse* look wholesome. "It's not an exaggeration to say that the worst, most vile, most perverse pornography is only a few click-click-clicks away from any child on the Internet," he said.

Supporters of the new law argued that freedom of speech was not absolute. Over the years, the courts had allowed the government to regulate speech in cases involving its "compelling interest" in protecting minors. The Supreme Court also had approved regulations to shield minors from "indecent" broadcasts such as George Carlin's famous "seven dirty words" monologue, in which he repeated seven curse words and commented on why they are considered too "bad" to be heard on network television.

Opponents, however, denounced the new law as an unconstitutional restriction on free speech. Hard-core pornography, which came under the legal heading of "obscenity," remains illegal. The government, they said, should enforce existing regulations rather than create a new law that could be used to censor everything from risqué pictures of celebrities to information about safe sex. The CDA, they said, was clearly unconstitutional.

But was it?

Over the years, the courts had allowed the government to regulate some communications mediums more heavily than others. Because radio and television flowed out to innocent bystanders and used limited airwaves, they could be more strictly controlled than books and newspapers. The FCC not only "limits" the airwaves, but it also licenses the airways, which effectively controls who can use them—and how.

Reno v. *ACLU* raised the question of whether the Internet was more like print or broadcasting. Plaintiffs argued that the Internet was more like print because users made conscious choices with every click of the mouse and so were rarely surprised by content. The government, on the other hand, maintained that the sounds and images of the Internet made it more like broadcasting, and hence could be regulated. Over the years, the Supreme Court had established a "spectrum of control" for the media. Because television and radio radiated out to "innocent bystanders," including young children who could not read, they were considered more "invasive" than newspapers and books.

But, even though free speech was more highly protected in print than in broadcasting, the courts had upheld statutes banning the sale of pornographic magazines to minors. Since laws prevented stores from selling magazines like *Playboy* or *Penthouse* to minors, supporters of the CDA believed that similar regulations should apply to the Internet.

NOT PORNOGRAPHERS
None of the plaintiffs in the ACLU suit, however, dealt in pornography. Instead, many were nonprofit organizations that provided information about safe sex or birth control that they said could be beneficial, rather than harmful, to minors.

A second group of plaintiffs headed by the American Library Association (ALA), which included companies such as Microsoft and CompuServe, maintained that technological solutions, such as filters, made the CDA unnecessary. Furthermore, they said, the filters could screen out pornography from abroad, estimated at about 40 percent of the total, which would not be affected by the statute.

As the consolidated suit awaited trial, opponents of the CDA displayed images of blue ribbons on their Web sites as symbols of free speech. On March 21, 1996, the event some called the "Cyberlaw Trial of the Century" began in a federal courthouse in Philadelphia not far from the historic Liberty Bell.

The three judges sat behind computer monitors installed specifically for the trial. Both sides gave the judges demonstrations of what one observer dubbed "Internet 101." Plaintiffs spoke about how the CDA would affect them personally.

In considering the case, the judges pondered the question of just what the new law would cover. Did the CDA target only pornography, as the government said? Or was it so "overbroad" and "vague," as the plaintiffs contended, that it would reduce the Internet to only what was fit for children?

On June 11, 1996, the three-judge panel issued its ruling, finding the CDA unconstitutional. The government appealed the case to the Supreme Court. The nation's top court agreed to hear the case.

CONSTITUTIONAL MUSTER

For the Communications Decency Act to pass constitutional muster, the government would need to show that it was "narrowly tailored" and served a "compelling interest." Although some experts hailed technological solutions such as filters as the most "narrowly tailored" option, the government said they were problematic, unable to keep up with the flow of new sites in cyberspace. The Justice Department argued that the CDA was the best option for meeting the government's "compelling interest" in protecting minors.

Lawyers on the other side of the case, however, maintained that the CDA offered neither the clarity nor the narrowness required of criminal statute restricting free speech. Moreover the nature of the Internet often made it difficult, if not impossible, to screen for age. In an earlier landmark case, the Supreme Court had ruled that government could not restrict the free-speech rights of adults to protect children. This, Justice Felix Frankfurter wrote, would "burn the house to roast the pig."

In lively oral arguments on March 19, 1997, the Supreme Court searched for metaphors for the Internet. Justice Stephen Breyer compared the new medium to the telephone. Would it be fair, he wondered, for teenagers who bragged about their sexual experiences online to be charged with a criminal offense while those who conducted similar conversations by phone faced no such penalties?

No, a majority of the justices decided. On June 26, 1997, the Supreme Court declared the CDA unconstitutional. Awarding the Internet the highest level of First Amendment protection, the Court criticized the CDA for its breadth.

ASSOCIATE JUSTICE STEPHEN BREYER HAD BEEN ON THE COURT FOR THREE YEARS WHEN THE COMMUNICATIONS DECENCY ACT WAS FIRST HEARD.

In the years following *Reno* v. *ACLU*, supporters of government regulation have drafted more narrowly tailored legislation. They have won some challenges and lost others. Increasingly, policymakers are looking at educational and technological solutions as well as legislation to protect kids online.

Even so, the influence of *Reno* v. *ACLU* remains a landmark. Policymakers are still debating how to protect both free speech and the well-being of minors. Through the ACLU, teens made their voices heard in *Reno* v. *ACLU*. Now it's time for a new generation of cyber-savvy youth to join the debate.

one
Two Different Experiences

One February Day In 1996, sixteen-year-old Rheana Parrenas got a call from Wildcat Press publisher Patricia Nell Warren.

"Would you be interested in contributing an affidavit to the court?" asked Warren, one of the plaintiffs in the American Civil Liberty Union's case to overturn the new Communications Decency Act (CDA).

Parrenas said yes. She knew the case would be a historic one for the future of cyberspace.

At the time, the Internet was so new it seemed like something out of a science-fiction novel. With a click of the button, Parrenas, who had formerly written for a college literary magazine, could reach readers from around the world.

Like most of the other teenagers who contributed affidavits in the case, Parrenas knew Warren as the copublisher of YouthArts, a new electronic publication for gay and lesbian teens. During YouthArts workshops, the teenagers learned how to lay out Web pages and surf the Web.

A self-described Filipina bisexual, Parrenas had found a sense of community online, through chat rooms for gay youth, which she hadn't found elsewhere. After coming out of the closet at school, she had gotten a harassing phone call about her homosexuality. Writing gave her a way to channel her emotions.

WILDCAT PRESS PUBLISHER PATRICIA NELL WARREN WAS ONE OF THE PLAIN-
TIFFS IN THE CASE TO OVERTURN THE COMMUNICATIONS DECENCY ACT.

Because her poems for YouthArts dealt with issues of
sexuality, she worried that they might be considered
"indecent" or "patently offensive" under the new CDA.
One poem, "Sister," involved child prostitution. Another,
"6 minutes," concerned a rape. Yet another, "Baby-Baby
Dyke" used the phrase "spit swapping" to describe
kissing. Even though it contained no explicit sexuality,
she wondered if "Baby-Baby Dyke" would be considered

"indecent" simply because it involved a lesbian relationship.

Warren put Parrenas in touch with Ann Beeson, the ACLU lawyer in charge of most of the affidavits for the case. Beeson explained that an affidavit was a statement that could be "sworn" by including certain language about its truthfulness and having it notarized. Parrenas got to work on her statement.

"I feel it to be important that my work is available for other teenagers, especially those who can identify with its subject matter," she wrote. "I feel that a quantity of my poems, particularly those published in YouthArts, reinforces the fundamental idea of not being alone, of not being 'the only one.'"

Once Parrenas finished writing her affidavit, Beeson gave her the ACLU's Federal Express number so she wouldn't have to pay for postage. Parrenas was flattered by the attention of an organization as well-known as the ACLU.

Several months passed before the case came to trial. During that time, Parrenas prepared for her participation in the Academic Decathlon, a national competition that included a different thematic section each year. The topic for 1996 was the "information superhighway."

Flipping through the Academic Decathlon study guide, Parrenas came upon a familiar name: Ann Beeson. While other students were learning about *Reno v. ACLU* from the study guide, Parrenas knew about it from real life.

14

"It was certainly exciting to be part of the legal system, much more satisfying and more real than any high school Mock Trial Competition!" she said. A verdict was still months away.

LEA'S STORY

Not all young people shared Parrenas's positive view of free speech on the Internet. For ten-year-old Lea, the Internet was anything but the innocent fun she thought it would be.

Shortly after the American Civil Liberties Union (ACLU) filed its suit in 1996, Lea signed onto the Internet for the first time. She logged into a children's chat room to play checkers with other kids in the hopes of earning her Girl Scout merit badge in computers. Within minutes of entering the children's chat room, Lea got a message from someone trying to engage her in a conversation of a sexual nature.

Lea was so shocked, she screamed to her mother. Lea's mother contacted their Internet server, Prodigy, which responded quickly by setting up an alert button for the children's area. She also contacted the news media.

On the morning of March 7, 1996, Senator James Exon heard the story about Lea on his car radio. Because the mother and daughter lived in the Washington, D.C., area, he set up a meeting with them. That same afternoon, he told their story on the floor of the U.S. Senate. He identified ten-year-old Lea only by her first name.

Senator Exon, the guiding force behind the CDA, spoke of how Lea reminded him of his own two ten-year-old granddaughters. "Mr. President, Lea's story demonstrates and illustrates better than anything else that I know of that there are, indeed, real dangers on the Internet, especially for children and especially with the interactive computer services that are available."

Senator Exon lauded Prodigy for acting quickly but insisted that the Internet servers alone could not protect kids from smut on the Internet. Government needed to step in. He was confident the courts would uphold the constitutionality of the Communications Decency Act.

TWO SIDES OF THE CASE

Ten-year-old Lea and sixteen-year-old Rheana Parrenas represented the two sides of *Reno* v. *ACLU*. On the one hand, kids like Lea wanted to be protected from unwanted material on the Internet. On the other hand, teens like Parrenas believed they should be able to express themselves freely.

Would one minor's rights need to be sacrificed to protect the other's? The answer would be up to the Supreme Court.

TWO
"INDECENCY" THROUGH THE AGES

LONG BEFORE THE BIRTH OF THE INTERNET, erotic frescoes adorned ancient Rome.

They went uncensored, as did bawdy songs and ribald tales, because rulers worried less about "smut," as we call it today, than about works that threatened their own political or religious authority. In medieval Europe, just calling the king a fool could result in death.

Religions varied in their response to sexually explicit works. The strict Puritans of Massachusetts passed a law in 1711 against obscenity, but it targeted religious, rather than secular, speech. Erotic publications such as Benjamin Franklin's "Letter of Advice to a Young Man on Choosing a Mistress" circulated freely throughout the thirteen colonies.

By 1788, the colonists had broken free from Britain and adopted their own Constitution. The question of just what was obscene never entered into the deliberations leading up to the ratification of the Bill of Rights in 1791.

Founding Father James Madison wrote amendments calling for the protection of free speech at the state as well as the federal level. But the shy and intellectual Madison won only a partial victory. The Senate approved his amendment for free speech at the federal, but not the state, level.

EROTICA WAS NOT CENSORED IN COLONIAL TIMES. EVEN BEN FRANKLIN
PUBLISHED SUCH MATERIAL.

The First Amendment reads: "Congress shall make no law respecting an establishment of religion, or prohibiting the free exercise thereof, or abridging the freedom of speech, or of the press; or the right of the people peaceably to assemble, and to petition the Government for a redress of grievances."

SUBJECT TO INTERPRETATION

Because the Founding Fathers never spelled out exactly what they meant by free speech, the task of interpreting the First Amendment fell to the courts. Often judges have disagreed with each other. One judge's idea of "fine art" might be another's view of "pornography." Also, what is scandalous for one generation might be considered tame by the next.

"Absolutists" on the Supreme Court have pointed to such problems to argue the First Amendment prohibits *any* restriction on free speech. But their colleagues have overruled them, establishing a set of legal precedents. The Supreme Court has ruled that certain types of speech, including "libel" and "defamation," "fighting words," and words that incite "imminent lawless action" are not protected by the Constitution.

To pass constitutional muster, laws restricting free speech must meet two conditions. First, the government needs to show a "compelling interest" for its restrictions. Second, laws curbing free speech must be "narrowly tailored" so that only the problematic areas are affected.

As an example of "compelling interest," Congress has pointed to its need to protect children from pornography. The word "pornography," however, is more of a popular term than a legal one. Instead, the courts have used the terms "indecency" and "obscenity" to guide them in what has turned out to be a difficult task.

VICTORIAN ERA

In the mid-nineteenth century, the invention of photography raised new concerns about sexually explicit material. Nude photos found their way through the federal mails to soldiers on the front lines of the Civil War. In 1865, Congress passed a law to curb obscenity through the federal mails, but the law was largely ineffective. A new movement sprang up for a tougher law, due to the efforts of one man—Anthony Comstock.

Born in New Canaan, Connecticut, in 1844, Comstock grew up in a New England farming family deeply steeped in Puritan discipline. During the Civil War, he enlisted in the Union army, where he found himself deeply disturbed by the drinking, gambling, and loose sexual behavior of his fellow soldiers.

After the Civil War, he established the New York Society for the Suppression of Vice. His crusade for "moral purity" fit right in with the times. Many medical experts and community leaders of the era warned that the "secret vice" of masturbation led to insanity and lack of virility.

In Victorian England, meanwhile, a judge offered the first legal definition of "obscenity." In the famous 1868 case of *Regina* v. *Hicklin*, Judge Alexander Cockburn defined "obscenity" as the tendency of any portion of the material to "deprave and corrupt those whose minds are open to such immoral influences."

Comstock led the United States in its adoption of the *Hicklin* standard. His intense lobbying effort in Washington, D.C., led to the passage of a new anti-obscenity statute, known as the Comstock Act, signed into law on March 3, 1873. The new law criminalized not only sexually explicit material but also information and products dealing with birth control and abortion. The government appointed Comstock a special agent to the office of the Postmaster General, giving him the power to inspect any article of mail and to arrest, without warrant, anyone whose correspondence did not meet with his approval.

As time went on, Comstock turned his attention to an increasingly wide array of targets, including medical textbooks and psychological studies. Many of his old supporters turned against him. The times had changed. Comstock died in 1915, a hero to some, a villain to others.

ANTHONY COMSTOCK, WHO ESTABLISHED THE NEW YORK SOCIETY FOR THE SUPPRESSION OF VICE, PERSONIFIED THE ANTI-OBSCENITY MOVEMENT IN THE UNITED STATES DURING THE NINETEENTH CENTURY. IT WAS AS A RESULT OF COMSTOCK'S EFFORTS THAT THE SALE OF BIRTH CONTROL (AND EVEN INFORMATION ABOUT IT) BECAME ILLEGAL IN 1873.

A "CHILD'S LIBRARY"

Even before Comstock's death, some people had begun to question the "deprave and corrupt" standard. In 1913, New York federal judge Learned Hand argued that the reading material of adults should not be limited to a "child's library."

Still, *Hicklin* remained the national standard until the 1957 case of *Butler* v. *Michigan* dismantled it. Alfred Butler had been convicted in a state court for selling a novel containing erotic elements to an adult. Michigan's obscenity statute echoed the *Hicklin* standard in its prohibition of material that might lead to the "corruption of the morals of youth."

Lawyers for Butler argued that the censorship standard for adults could not turn on what might corrupt minors. The state maintained that the statute protected the general welfare of society.

Justice Felix Frankfurter sided with Butler. Adults could

not be reduced to reading what was fit for children. "This is to burn the house to roast the pig," he wrote in his decision.

OBSCENITY AND THE FIRST AMENDMENT

Also in 1957, the Supreme Court grappled with an important question: Was obscenity protected or not protected by the First Amendment? For centuries, judges had avoided directly addressing the question. That changed with the landmark case of *Roth* v. *United States*.

Samuel Roth had been convicted under the Comstock Act of mailing obscene books, circulars, and advertising material. In upholding Roth's conviction, Justice William Brennan held that obscenity was not entitled to First Amendment protection.

> All ideas having even the slightest redeeming social importance—unorthodox ideas, controversial ideas, even ideas hateful to the prevailing climate of opinion—have the full protection of the guarantees. But implicit in the history of the First Amendment is the rejection of obscenity as utterly without redeeming social importance.

Justice Brennan held that sex and obscenity were not synonymous. In a quote that would become famous, Justice Brennan described sex as "a great and mysterious motive force in human life." Obscenity, on the other hand, was material whose "dominant theme taken as a whole appeals to the prurient interest" to the "average person applying community standards." By prurient, he meant, "material having a tendency to excite lustful thoughts." Later court rulings would determine that "prurient" was not normal lust.

Absolutist Justices William O. Douglas and Hugo Black reacted angrily to the *Roth* decision. Justice Black lamented that the Court was being turned into a "Supreme Board of Censors."

GROPING FOR A NEW DEFINITION

Lower-court judges had so much trouble interpreting the new *Roth* guidelines that the Supreme Court became flooded with cases. The Court initiated a new tradition—movie day—to screen questionable films.

After the screening of one such movie in 1964, Justice Potter Stewart argued in the case of *Jacobellis* v. *Ohio*, that only hard-core pornography should be considered obscene. But what was "hard-core pornography"? He couldn't say beyond, "I know it when I see it."

Stewart's famous line—"I know it when I see it"—pointed to the difficulties the courts were having defining obscenity. Pornographers started throwing in lines from Shakespeare or other ploys to satisfy the requirement of "redeeming social importance." In one movie, for instance, an actor playing the role of a psychologist concludes, "And so our nymphomaniac subject was never cured."

In the early 1970s, the political makeup of the Supreme Court became more conservative when President Richard Nixon appointed four new justices: Chief Justice Warren Burger, Justice William Rehnquist, Justice Harry Blackmun, and Justice Lewis Powell. Chief Justice Burger, who replaced liberal Chief Justice Earl Warren, saw an opportunity to redefine obscenity.

In the 1973 case of *Miller* v. *California*, Chief Justice Burger redefined obscenity, which he categorized according to three tests:

• whether the average person applying contemporary community standards would find that the work, taken as a whole, appeals to the prurient interest,

• whether the work depicts or describes, in a patently offensive way, sexual conduct . . . specifically defined by the applicable state laws, and
• whether the work, taken as a whole, lacks serious literary, artistic, political, or scientific value.

Chief Justice Burger's historic decision asserted that works could be gauged by local, rather than national, standards. The Chief Justice saw no reason why "the people of Maine or Mississippi" should "accept public depiction of conduct found tolerable in Las Vegas or New York City. . . ."

Justice Brennan, who had come to regret his ruling in the *Roth* case, strongly disagreed with the decision. In his dissent, Brennan argued that the meaning of concepts such as "prurient interest," "patent offensiveness," and "serious literary value" varied with the "experience outlook, and even the idiosyncrasies of the person defining them."

HARMFUL TO MINORS

Could material that met the *Miller* test for adults be held to a different standard to protect children? Yes, the courts ruled in a variety of cases in the second half of the twentieth century. For instance, the Supreme Court took steps to curb child pornography to prevent children from being exploited. In addition, it also ruled on a number of cases involving material deemed "harmful to minors."

In *Ginsberg* v. *New York* in 1968, the Supreme Court decided that states could restrict material to children that was legal for adults. Sam Ginsberg, the owner of a luncheonette and stationery store in Long Island, was arrested for selling two "girlie" magazines to a sixteen-year-old boy in violation of New York's "harmful to minors" statute. Since the magazines would not be considered obscene for adults, lawyers for Ginsberg argued that the

New York law violated the constitutional rights of minors. The Supreme Court, however, disagreed.

The *Ginsberg* decision set forth the notion of "variable obscenity." Justice Brennan held that the state had "an independent interest in the well-being of youth" and so could protect minors from unwelcome speech.

"SEVEN DIRTY WORDS" CASE

Next, in the famous "seven dirty words" case, the *Federal Communications Commission* v. *Pacifica* in 1978, the Supreme Court upheld the power of the government to restrict "indecent" but not necessarily "obscene" material on the airwaves. The case grew out of a mid-afternoon radio broadcast on October 30, 1973, of a twelve-minute monologue, "Filthy Words," by comedian George Carlin.

Until this historic case, the courts had viewed "indecency" as synonymous with "obscenity." In 1995, the Federal Communications Commission (FCC) offered a new definition of "indecency" as "the exposure of children to language that describes in terms patently offensive . . . sexual or excretory activities and organs." Even works with "literary, artistic, or scientific value" and no "prurient" interest could be regulated to protect minors from "obnoxious gutter language."

After receiving a complaint from a listener, the FCC faulted Pacifica for airing "indecent" language at a time when children might be listening. The monologue repeats the words over and over again to poke fun at society's taboo against them. Pacifica appealed the decision, sending the case to court. In 1978, the Supreme Court ruled in a narrow 5 to 4 decision that the broadcast media could be regulated because of their "uniquely pervasive presence in the lives of all Americans."

Carlin criticized the decision, saying that anyone offended by his monologue could have simply turned off the

GEORGE CARLIN'S MONOLOGUE

Comedian George Carlin analyzes swear words like he's a linguist from Mars.

With his characteristic anti-establishment humor, the bearded, pony-tailed comic pokes fun at society's taboos. Religion, he says, has imbued words dealing with sex and bodily functions with shame, guilt, and embarrassment.

In 1972, Carlin released his famous monologue "Seven Words You Can Never Say on Television," showcasing his trademark fondness for wordplay. The following year he recorded a sequel, "Filthy Words," on his comedy album *Occupation: Foole*.

"Filthy Words" begins with Carlin musing about the swear words that are okay to say on the airwaves. Then he lists the ones that aren't. "Those are the ones that will curve your spine, grow hair on your hands and maybe even bring us, God help us, peace without honor and a bourbon," he says.

One word, for instance, is only "50 percent dirty—dirty half the time, depending on what you mean by it." Middle-class women, he says, use another one of the words whenever they drop something. Yet another term can be used either to describe lovemaking or to hurt someone.

At about two o'clock in the afternoon on Tuesday, October 30, 1973, a New York radio station, WBAI, broadcast "Filthy Words" as part of a show about contemporary attitudes toward language. Before airing the segment, WBAI, which was owned by the Pacifica Foundation, warned listeners that the twelve-minute piece contained "sensitive language that might be regarded as offensive to some."

A motorist driving with his son didn't like what he heard. The father wrote a letter of complaint to the FCC, setting off the famous case of *Federal Communications Commission* v. *Pacifica*.

Even though Carlin lost the case, the publicity might have given his career a boost. In the midst of the litigation in 1975, he hosted the first-ever broadcast of *Saturday Night Live*. He went on to star in his own sitcom and rack up four Grammy awards for comedy albums.

When shock jock Howard Stern made headlines in 2004 for obscenity infractions, reporters turned to the sixty-six-year-old Carlin for comment. Predictably, Carlin blamed "religious superstition."

Over the years, fans have suggested new offerings to Carlin's collection of "impolite words." When his list reached 2,000, he made it into a T-shirt, which he sells on his Web site. Carlin's Web site also includes a transcript of his "Filthy Words" monologue and excerpts from the court decision. His list of "impolite words," meanwhile, has grown to 2,443.

COMEDIAN GEORGE CARLIN'S "FILTHY WORDS" MONOLOGUE IN 1973 LED TO
A RULING THAT THE FEDERAL GOVERNMENT COULD RESTRICT "INDECENT"
MATERIAL ON THE AIRWAVES, EVEN IF IT WAS NOT OBSCENE.

radio. "There are two knobs on the radio and television," he
said. "One turns it off, and the other changes the station."

Justice John Paul Stevens disagreed with Carlin's
logic. "To say that one may avoid further offense by

turning off the radio when he hears indecent language is like saying that the remedy for an assault is to run away after the first blow," he wrote.

In a particularly controversial section of his decision, Justice Stevens argued that indecency lay at the periphery of the First Amendment. "There are few, if any thoughts, that cannot be expressed by the use of less offensive language," he said.

Still, Justice Stevens emphasized the "narrowness" of his ruling. His decision, he said, was limited to the "specific factual context" of the case at hand. He left any applications of the decision to the future.

"DIAL-A-PORN"

In the early 1980s, Congress began drafting legislation to protect children from "obscene or indecent" commercial phone sex lines known as "dial-a-porn." The 1988 dial-a-porn bill, which banned the services, came in response to complaints from citizens whose children had run up massive phone bills. Minors could access the 900 numbers, which charged two dollars or more per minute, without their parents' knowledge.

Critics argued that the legislation was unconstitutional because it unfairly restricted access to adults. In the 1989 case of *Sable Communications* v. *FCC*, the Supreme Court agreed. Indecency could be "channeled" but not banned. It was another case of "burning the house to roast the pig."

Congress redrafted the legislation. The new law called for more narrowly tailored measures such as credit card verification and "blocking" technology to prevent minors from being able to access the sex lines.

In 1992, the Supreme Court upheld the constitutionality of the dial-a-porn legislation. In its decision, the court noted the "compelling interest" of the government to protect minors from indecent speech.

BIRTH OF THE INTERNET

Could similar regulations against "indecency" be applied to the new information highway? Originally a system of computer networks developed by the United States Department of Defense, the Internet took off as a popular medium in the early 1990s with the innovation of "hypertext" by English software designer Tim Berners-Lee. A diverse group of people—including some pornographers—flocked to the Web. In 1994, the United States Postal Inspector filed criminal charges against the husband-wife pornography team of Robert and Carleen Thomas for violating the United States obscenity laws. The Thomases were found guilty, indicating that the government's long-standing laws against obscenity could be applied to the Internet.

But what about "indecent" material that fell short of the legal definition of "obscenity"? "Indecent," as defined by the *Pacifica* case, could include material with serious value and no prurient interest. "Obscenity," on the other hand, usually applied to hard-core pornography. Before long, that question of whether or not to regulate "indecency" on the Internet would give rise to the case of *Reno* v. *ACLU*.

Three
The Communications Decency Act

AS THE new information superhighway took off in the mid-1990s, lawmakers began to hear about its "gritty roadside attractions."

Cyberporn became a hot topic of concern. In just a few short years, the Internet had experienced astronomical growth, transforming itself from a small research network to a virtual marketplace that offered everything from pizza delivery to hard-core and soft-core pornography. In 1995, screening technology for the Internet was just getting started.

For Senator J. James Exon of Nebraska, the impetus for creating a new set of "rules of the road" for cyberspace came after watching a television special about online pedophiles. In February of 1995, he filed his first version of the Communications Decency Act (CDA). Although existing laws governing child pornography and obscenity were already being applied to the Internet, Exon believed that more legislation was needed.

A former governor and owner of an office equipment company, the seventy-four-year-old Exon was known in the Senate as the voice of the heartland. *Politics in America*, a book produced by *Congressional Quarterly*, described Exon by saying, "It is hard to think of anyone else in the chamber who seems as attuned to the questions and concerns of the typical middle-American."

Like many concerned parents, Exon believed that the Internet needed to be made safe for children. He figured that, since the Internet used the phone lines, it could be regulated much like dial-a-porn. Exon's CDA became an amendment to the Telecommunications Act of 1996, a wide-ranging piece of legislation that included sections on cable television and the V-chip as well as Internet indecency.

At first, Exon's bill attracted little interest. Then, in early June, the senator showed colleagues his "blue book." A blue binder filled with pornographic images downloaded by the anti-pornography group Enough Is Enough, the "blue book" shocked fellow senators, garnering new support for the bill. Exon also drew support from conservative Christians and anti-pornography activists, including some feminists who believed that pornography hurt women.

Internet providers, on the other hand, opposed the bill because they worried that it would hold them criminally responsible. After listening to their concerns, Exon decided to exempt them from criminal liability because they performed a role similar to that of mail carriers. Only content providers would be prosecuted. The final version of the bill in the Senate imposed a $100,000 fine and two-year prison term on anyone who violated the regulations.

Civil libertarians sharply criticized the bill for including "indecency" along with "obscenity." The Supreme Court had ruled that, while obscenity was not protected by the Constitution, "indecency" was and so could be "channeled" but not banned. Exon's critics worried that the CDA would criminalize online discussions about safe sex, rape, homosexuality, and other important social issues. Ridding the Internet of "smut" would be like forcing all theaters to show "G-rated" movies, they said. Moreover, they complained that the bill's authors didn't understand the Internet or use it themselves.

NEBRASKA SENATOR J. JAMES EXON SPONSORED THE COMMUNICATIONS DECENCY ACT IN 1995.

Organizations such as the American Civil Liberties Union (ACLU) began lobbying Congress in the hopes of defeating the bill.

SENATOR LEAHY'S ALTERNATIVE
Senator Patrick Leahy of Vermont headed up the opposition to the Exon bill in the Senate. Known as the "cyber-senator," the fifty-five-year-old Leahy had quickly become a fan of the convenience of the Internet. His home in Vermont had only one television channel and was five miles away from the nearest newspaper source.

"I'm addicted to the Internet, I admit it," he wrote. "It has transformed the way I work as a senator, communicate with my children, and keep tabs on news and cultural developments."

Leahy offered an alternative to the Exon bill: a Justice Department study of the Internet to look into ways to improve law enforcement and empower parents. A former prosecutor, Leahy shared Exon's desire to protect children from hard-core pornography but objected to his inclusion of "indecency" along with "obscenity." The cybersenator's alternative drew widespread support from publishers, librarians, and civil liberties groups. Within a month, 35,000 people signed an online petition in favor of Leahy's proposed study.

On Wednesday, June 14, 1995, the Senate debated the CDA in a session carried live on C-SPAN. Time was evenly divided between the Exon and Leahy sides of the issue. The session began with a prayer from the chaplain read by Exon.

"Lord, give us courage to balance our reverence for freedom of speech with responsibility for what is said and depicted," read Exon. "Now guide the senators when they consider ways of controlling the pollution of computer communications and how to preserve one of our greatest resources: the minds of our children and the future and moral strength of our Nation. Amen."

Then Exon spoke in his own words. First, he argued that America's "electronic neighborhood" needed the same kind of protections as other communities.

"If in any American neighborhood an individual were distributing pornographic photos, cartoons, videos, and stories to children, or if someone were posting lewd photographs on lampposts and telephone polls for all to see, or if children were welcome to enter and browse adult book stores and triple X-rated video arcades, there would be public outrage," Exon said. "I suspect and I hope that most people, under those circumstances would immediately call

VERMONT SENATOR PATRICK LEAHY HEADED THE OPPOSITION AGAINST THE COMMUNICATIONS DECENCY ACT, ARGUING THAT IT WOULD RESTRICT SOCIALLY VALUABLE SPEECH AS WELL AS PORNOGRAPHY.

the police to arrest and charge any person responsible for such offenses."

"NOT TALKING ABOUT *PLAYBOY* AND *PENTHOUSE*"

Then Exon described how his colleagues had reacted with shock to the material in his "blue book." The blue binder, he said, contained photos and stories of torture, child abuse, and bestiality.

"Mr. President, it is no exaggeration to say that the most disgusting, repulsive pornography is only a few clicks away from any child with a computer," he declared. "I am not talking just about *Playboy* and *Penthouse* magazines. By comparison, those magazines pale in offensiveness with the other things that are readily available."

Exon closed his first speech by describing his efforts to balance respect for the Constitution with protection of American families. His legislation, he said, upheld the Constitutional rights of consenting adults.

Leahy's turn came next. The six-foot-four senator from Vermont spoke about how he, too, had been shocked by Exon's "blue book," which he had glimpsed over the shoulders of his shorter colleagues. But, he said, the Justice Department was already using existing laws to prosecute pedophiles and pornographers.

"Nobody in here would disagree with the fact that we want to keep hard-core pornography away from our children," he began. "If pornographers are out there, prosecute them. As a former prosecutor and as a parent, I find them the most disgusting people."

Leahy, however, argued that the CDA would affect socially valuable speech as well as pornography. For example, someone who belonged to a discussion group about rape could be prosecuted for downloading a graphic story from a fellow member. He noted that anyone who mentioned one of George Carlin's "seven dirty words" in an e-mail also could be subject to prosecution.

"AS IF . . . IN SUNDAY SCHOOL"

The law, Leahy said, would force users of computer e-mail and other network systems to speak as if they were in "Sunday school." Even anti-pornography activists could be found guilty of violating the law, he said. "If this amendment had been the law when my good friend from

Nebraska collected the materials in his blue notebook, he would have committed a felony," he announced.

The debate then swung back to the other side, with Exon's cosponsor, Senator Daniel Coats of Indiana, taking the floor. Coats began by speaking about the difficulty of balancing First Amendment rights with the protection of children.

Admitting his own difficulty with a VCR ("I have a blinking 12 I do not know how to get rid of," he said), Coats described children as the nation's computer experts. "The Internet is like taking a porn shop and putting it in the bedroom of your children and then saying, 'Do not look,'" he said.

Coats took issue with the criticism that the CDA would cripple the Internet. Pornographic magazine stores and telephone companies were alive and well despite regulations governing sexually explicit material to minors.

Next, Leahy's cosponsor, Senator Russell Feingold of Wisconsin, spoke. Feingold began by commending Exon for raising awareness about inappropriate material on the Internet. Still, Feingold said, the Supreme Court called for the "least restrictive" means of regulating speech so adults would not be reduced to what was appropriate for children. Cases involving the "seven dirty words" and "dial-a-porn" had called for restrictions rather than outright bans on indecency. The CDA, on the other hand, would have a "chilling effect" on constitutionally protected speech to adults, he said.

Feingold also argued that, because the Internet was unique, it could not be regulated like other technologies. Moreover, he said, "Users of the Internet and other on-line functions typically do not stumble across information, but go out surfing for materials on a particular subject."

The debate wound to a close with Senator Joseph Biden speaking of his concerns about the bill's constitutionality.

As the C-SPAN cameras rolled, the Senate voted on Exon's amendment. The clerk called the roll. The result was announced: yeas 84, nays 14. The CDA was headed for the House of Representatives.

MEDIA FIRESTORM

A flurry of media stories followed the Senate's approval of the Communications Decency Act.

On June 22, 1995, Senator Exon appeared on the *MacNeil-Lehrer News Hour* to debate Jerry Berman, the executive director of the Center for Democracy and Technology (CDT), one of the groups that would later become plaintiffs in *Reno* v. *ACLU*.

Although civil libertarian Berman agreed that child pornographers and pedophiles should be prosecuted, he disagreed with Exon's inclusion of "indecency" in the bill. If adults were having an online discussion about *Ulysses* and a sixteen-year-old logged on, they could be subject to prosecution, Berman said.

The moderator asked Exon if this were true. Exon replied that prosecution of such material was unlikely. As the debate progressed, Berman argued that the Internet was different from the U.S. mails or the telephone system because it involved more than just two people communicating with each other. He also pointed out that, since the Internet was a global rather than national medium, some of the pornography for Exon's "blue book" might have come from countries outside of the United States. People didn't come across the unexpected on the Internet as they did with radio or television. Hence, Berman believed that the government should have less control over the Internet than the broadcasting industry. Moreover, people needed to "come and get" whatever they wanted on the Web. "I understand it may be a few clicks away, but you have to come and get it," Berman said.

Jerry Berman, director of the Center for Democracy and Technology, is shown leaving federal court in Philadelphia on April 15, 1996. He testified against the Communications Decency Act.

Next, the debate turned to the First Amendment. Exon said that he wanted Berman and other civil libertarians to work with him rather than "hiding behind the old constitutional protection." He faulted civil libertarians like Berman for making it seem as if Founding Fathers such as Thomas Jefferson wanted to protect pornographers. Berman replied that he was proud to be associated with "the gang that goes back to Thomas Jefferson."

That same week, *Newsweek* ran an article highly critical of the Senate vote titled, "A Bad Day in Cyberspace: The Senate Takes a Sledgehammer to Our Communications Future." In it, writer Steven Levy wryly commented on the bill's inclusion of the word "annoying": "So much for most of my mail."

"I'm no prude," Levy quoted Exon as saying to him. He explained to Levy that he simply wanted to protect children. The *Newsweek* article credited Exon with jump-starting the creation of new family-friendly screening technologies. But it also faulted him for not understanding the Internet. "The issue of sexual content has been blown far out of proportion," Levy maintained.

In the last week of June, the media firestorm heated up when *Time* magazine released its controversial cover story, "CYBERPORN." The magazine's subhead declared, "EXCLUSIVE: A new study shows how pervasive and wild it really is. Can we protect our kids—and free speech?" The cover photo showed a child awash in the eerie glow of a computer screen.

Marty Rimm, a thirty-year-old undergraduate at Carnegie Mellon University, had given *Time* exclusive information from his study, "Marketing Pornography on the Information Superhighway," to be published by the *Georgetown Law Journal*. The Rimm study claimed that the most popular images online were hard-core porn such as bondage, sadomasochism, and bestiality. Writer Philip Elmer-DeWitt described these offerings by saying: "Suffice it to say that they all end in exclamation points, many include such phrases as 'nailed to a table!' and none can be printed in *Time*."

Soon after the article appeared, a study came out attacking Rimm's survey for exaggerating the extent of sex in cyberspace. Donna Hoffman and Thomas Novak, associate professors of management at Vanderbilt University, faulted Rimm—and *Time*—for drawing conclusions about cyberspace in general from an analysis primarily of private adult-oriented bulletin boards, which are off-limits to minors and require credit cards for payment. In actuality, they wrote, less than half of one percent of the messages on the Internet were associated with newsgroups that contained pornographic imagery.

Hoffman and Novak also argued that Rimm's study should have been submitted for peer review and that *Time* should have sought the opinions of objective experts. *Time*, they said, also erred by referring to Rimm's work as the "Carnegie Mellon study" rather than the work of one individual. "The magazine behaved irresponsibly in accepting statements made by Rimm in his manuscript at face value," Hoffman and Novak wrote.

Elmer-Dewitt responded to the controversy in a July 24, 1995, article in *Time*, "Fire Storm on the Computer Nets." He acknowledged the critique by Hoffman and Novak as well as Rimm's growing credibility problems in light of new information showing he had privately published a work titled *The Pornographer's Handbook: How to Exploit Women, Dupe Men, and Make Lots of Money*. Not surprisingly, some civil libertarians had accused *Time* of contributing to a mood of "popular hysteria."

Letters to the editor illustrated the intensity of public concern. "If we lose our kids to cyberporn, free speech won't matter," one reader wrote.

DISAGREEMENT IN THE HOUSE

House Speaker Newt Gingrich, a brash, high-profile force in American politics, in 1995 told the media that he believed the CDA was unconstitutional. Although an old-fashioned conservative on many matters, Gingrich, a Republican from Georgia, extolled technology as a key to America's future. He also had written a science-fiction novel, *1945*, which contained scenes that might be considered "indecent" under the new bill.

At first, the House seemed to be following Gingrich's lead. Members of the House were younger than their counterparts in the Senate and more familiar with the Internet. The House voted against giving the Federal Communications Commission the power to regulate the Internet.

Then the direction shifted. Conservative Republican Henry Hyde of Illinois amended the Comstock Act of 1873 to cover computers. Pro-choice activists reacted angrily to the amendment to the CDA, which they believed criminalized discussions about birth control. Hyde, however, said the provision applied only to using a computer to buy or sell abortion drugs and devices.

PROTEST

On the opposite end of the political spectrum, several communications and civil liberties groups came together to oppose the CDA. This new coalition found the Internet a highly effective organizing tool. Mass e-mails propelled members to action.

On Tuesday, December 12, 1995, the online coalition waged an Internet Day of Protest. Participants called and faxed key members of the Senate and House of Representatives to express their opposition to the Communications Decency Act. Organizers estimated that more than 50,000 faxes and phone calls were received by Congress on that one day.

REVIVAL AND PASSAGE

In the House-Senate Conference Committee, attempts at compromise failed. The committee rejected a proposal to substitute "variable obscenity" for the more sweeping category of "indecency." The "variable obscenity" standard would have provided exemptions for works that lacked prurient value and/or had serious scientific, literary, artistic, or political value.

As finally approved, the CDA made it a crime to use the Internet to: 1) transmit "indecent" material knowing the recipient is under eighteen, or 2) knowingly send "patently offensive" material "as measured by community standards, sexual or excretory activities or organs" over the Internet to a specific person or person under eighteen years of age, or 3) knowingly display such patently offensive material to anyone under the age of eighteen.

The "patently offensive" clause harked back to the famous "seven dirty words" case of 1978. The CDA carried a "good faith" exemption for people who took steps to prevent minors from accessing "indecent" or "patently offensive" material. It also carried a $250,000 fine and/or jail sentences of up to two years.

Recognizing the possibility of a constitutional challenge, the bill included a clause outlining a procedure for expedited legal review. If the act were challenged, it would go first to a three-judge panel, then straight to the Supreme Court.

On February 1, 1996, both houses of Congress overwhelmingly approved the entire Telecommunications Reform Act, including the CDA. On Thursday, February 8, 1996, President Bill Clinton signed the CDA into law.

ACLU FILES SUIT

On that same day, the American Civil Liberties Union (ACLU) filed suit in the Third Circuit Court of Appeals to overturn the CDA. For months, the organization had worked behind the scenes to put together a coalition of twenty groups opposed to the new law.

The coalition included a variety of AIDS education, human rights, civil liberties, media, and reproductive health groups, including the Critical Path AIDS Project,

THROUGH THE COURT SYSTEM

First Stop: State Court
Almost all cases (about 95 percent) start in state courts. These courts go by various names, depending on the state in which they operate: circuit, district, municipal, county, or superior. The case is tried and decided by a judge, a panel of judges, or a jury.

The side that loses can then appeal to the next level.

First Stop: Federal Court
U.S. DISTRICT COURT—About 5 percent of cases begin their journey in federal court. Most of these cases concern federal laws, the U.S. Constitution, or disputes that involve two or more states. They are heard in one of the ninety-four U.S. district courts in the nation.

U.S. COURT OF INTERNATIONAL TRADE—Federal court cases involving international trade appear in the U.S. Court of International Trade.

U.S. CLAIMS COURT—The U.S. Claims Court hears federal cases that involve more than $10,000, Indian claims, and some disputes with government contractors.

The loser in federal court can appeal to the next level.

Appeals: State Cases
Forty states have appeals courts that hear cases that have come from the state courts. In states without an appeals court, the case goes directly to the state supreme court.

Appeals: Federal Cases
U.S. CIRCUIT COURT—Cases appealed from U.S. district courts go to U.S. circuit courts of appeals. There are twelve circuit courts that handle cases from throughout the

nation. Each district court and every state and territory are assigned to one of the twelve circuits. Appeals in a few state cases—those that deal with rights guaranteed by the U.S. Constitution—are also heard in this court.

U.S. COURT OF APPEALS—Cases appealed from the U.S. Court of International Trade and the U.S. Claims Court are heard by the U.S. Court of Appeals for the Federal Circuit. Among the cases heard in this court are those involving patents and minor claims against the federal government.

Further Appeals: State Supreme Court

Cases appealed from state appeals courts go to the highest courts in the state—usually called supreme court. In New York, the state's highest court is called the court of appeals. Most state cases do not go beyond this point.

Final Appeals: U.S. Supreme Court

The U.S. Supreme Court is the highest court in the country. Its decision on a case is the final word. The Court decides issues that can affect every person in the nation. It has decided cases on slavery, abortion, school segregation, and many other important issues.

The Court selects the cases it will hear—usually around one hundred each year. Four of the nine justices must vote to consider a case in order for it to be heard. Almost all cases have been appealed from the lower courts (either state or federal).

Most people seeking a decision from the Court submit a petition for *certiorari*. Certiorari means that the case will be moved from a lower court to a higher court for review. The Court receives about nine thousand of these requests annually. The petition outlines the case and gives reasons why the Court should review it.

In rare cases, for example *New York Times* v. *United States*, an issue must be decided immediately. When such a case is of national importance, the Court allows it to bypass the usual lower court system and hears the case directly.

To win a spot on the Court's docket, a case must fall within one of the following categories:

- Disputes between states and the federal government or between two or more states. The Court also reviews cases involving ambassadors, consuls, and foreign ministers.

- Appeals from state courts that have ruled on a federal question.

- Appeals from federal appeals courts (about two-thirds of all requests fall into this category).

Electronic Frontier Foundation, Electronic Privacy Information Center (EPIC), Human Rights Watch, National Writers Union, Planned Parenthood Federation of America, and Wildcat Press.

Because the ACLU's suit involved a national law, the organization could file its suit in any federal court. It chose the third circuit court in Philadelphia because it had ruled favorably on another case involving First Amendment rights. In a case involving "dial-a-porn," Judge Dolores Sloviter maintained that the decision to censor children should rest with parents, not the state.

The ACLU believed that the same argument applied to the Internet. Arguing that the CDA was unconstitutionally "vague" and "overbroad," the plaintiffs eagerly awaited their day in court.

four
A CASE BEGINS

February 8, 1996, went down in the history of cyberspace as Black Thursday. To protest the president's signing of the CDA, civil libertarians turned their Web pages black. In addition, they displayed images of blue ribbons on their Web sites as symbols of free speech.

On the other side of the political divide, supporters of the CDA launched their own ribbon campaigns. White ribbons stood for responsible speech. "While the CDA is certainly not perfect, it is a step in the right direction," the campaign stated on its Web site. The green ribbon movement, in turn, called for Internet users to refrain from "vulgar, profane, violent, and insulting" communications.

The day after President Clinton signed the CDA into law, Attorney General Janet Reno wrote a letter to Vice President Al Gore, informing him that the Department of Justice would not defend the constitutionality of the abortion-related provisions of the CDA. Enforcing the provisions "plainly would be unconstitutional," she wrote.

FAST TRACK CASE
On the legal front, the case against the CDA got off to a quick start. Because the name of the party that files suit comes first, the case began as *ACLU* v. *Reno*. The order changed when the government appealed the district court's decision to the Supreme Court.

ANTHONY COPPOLINO WAS THE LEAD LAWYER FOR THE DEPARTMENT OF JUSTICE IN THE *RENO* V. *ACLU* CASE. HE IS PICTURED (RIGHT) WITH HIS TEAM.

Behind the scenes, ACLU lawyer Ann Beeson handled most of the phone and e-mail contact with plaintiffs. An amateur pilot in her spare time, she was already an experienced navigator of the Internet. Christopher Hansen, an experienced litigator in his late forties, headed up the case.

On the other side, Anthony Coppolino, the lead lawyer for the Department of Justice, began preparing for the trial by buying himself a personal computer and surfing the Web. He punched in keywords like "xxx" and "porn" to see what kind of sexually explicit material would be available to minors. Later, working with an expert witness, he and his colleagues prepared a printout of these materials that went into a book of exhibits for the trial.

THE MAGICIAN'S FEAT

Teller, of the famous magic duo Penn and Teller, told ACLU lawyer Ann Beeson about a surprising—and almost magical—experience. In response to an ACLU call for action, he phoned the attorney general's office and spoke to Janet Reno herself. He followed up his phone conversation with a letter, which he shared with the ACLU:

TO: ATTORNEY GENERAL JANET RENO
FROM: TELLER
Dear Attorney General Reno,
    I spoke with you this afternoon briefly and not very articulately. It was quite startling to find you in and I'm not great at thinking on my feet.
    Please, please, I urge you not to stand behind the "decency" provisions of the telecom act. They limit our freedom of speech. That freedom protects us from tyranny. That freedom is a lot more important than keeping kids from visiting Adults Only web sites. Internet providers are now starting to offer services that suit families who wish to limit the kids' browsing. Sure, some kids will still sneak into areas they shouldn't. But I'd much rather have your expertise and energy directed against the guys who rape, kill, and steal; not waste it on mischievous kids reading and writing and looking at pictures.
    Jefferson would not be pleased to hear you ask our nation to limit our communications to topics suitable for children. He would understand that the Internet is a huge library created by adults for their use. Children have found their way in. If we prefer kids not to see grownup books, let us engineer ways to keep them out. But let us

not burn down the library or make it a criminal act to stock anything stronger than Dr. Seuss.

"They that can give up essential liberty to obtain a little temporary safety deserve neither liberty nor safety," wrote Benjamin Franklin in 1759. Even if censoring the Internet would actually reduce crime (and you are experienced enough to know in your heart it wouldn't), to do so would betray the men and women who have died for our freedom.

Please think about it. You are important. Don't let us down.

Respectfully,
TELLER

Coppolino, who was thirty-seven at the time, recognized the historic nature of the case. It would be the first to apply the indecency standard to the Internet. A former class president who thrived on the vigorous debate of the courtroom, he saw the high-profile *ACLU* v. *Reno* as a lawyer's dream case.

To help with the workload, Coppolino and colleague Jason Baron brought in fellow Department of Justice lawyers Patricia Russotto and Mary Kostel. Although Coppolino barely knew Patricia Russotto at the time, working together on the case fostered a special closeness. The two eventually got married.

When Russotto left the Department of Justice in 1999, after they were married, Coppolino joked at her going-away party, "Who says you can't meet a nice woman through porn on the Internet?"

TEMPORARY RESTRAINING ORDER

To prevent the CDA from taking effect even before the case was tried, the ACLU filed a motion for a temporary restraining order (TRO). Judge Sloviter assigned a district judge, Ronald Buckwalter, to hear the plaintiff's request for the TRO. Then a panel of three judges would hear the case itself.

In its motion for the TRO, the ACLU argued that the CDA failed to meet the two requirements needed to pass constitutional muster. First, the government lacked a "compelling interest" in protecting children from "indecency" on the Internet. The plaintiffs argued that such information could be beneficial, rather than harmful, to children.

Second, they said, the act failed to meet the "second prong" of being "narrowly tailored." Narrower alternatives, such as screening software, could be used to protect children on the Internet.

In addition, the plaintiffs argued that CDA would unfairly restrict material for the adult population and discriminate against the computer industry. Furthermore, the terms "indecency" and "patently offensive" were "unconstitutionally vague and overbroad."

Six days later, on February 14, 1996, the government filed its response. In its introduction, lawyers for the Department of Justice argued that the plaintiff's concerns were "wholly speculative." The act targeted pornography, not health or policy-related material related to sexual matters, they maintained.

"Because enjoining an Act of Congress is such an extraordinary step, plaintiffs' request for a TRO should be denied on this basis alone," the government's attorneys wrote.

Next, the brief took issue with the plaintiffs' argument that the CDA failed to satisfy the "compelling interest" and "narrowly tailored" requirements. It pointed out that cases dealing with dial-a-porn, child pornography, and pornographic magazines, as well as George Carlin's "seven dirty words," had established government's "compelling interest" in shielding minors from "indecency."

Furthermore, it said, the CDA allowed for content providers to post indecent messages as long as they took "reasonable and appropriate" measures to block access to children, thus satisfying the requirement of "least restrictive means." It also stated that voluntary measures by parents did not constitute a "least restrictive" alternative because government had "an independent interest in the well-being of its youth."

Finally, the brief argued that the CDA was not unconstitutionally "vague" or "overbroad." The Supreme Court, it said, had rejected the vagueness concerns of the Pacifica Foundation in the "seven dirty words" case. In addition,

JUDGE DOLORES K. SLOVITER, TRAILBLAZER

Judge Dolores K. Sloviter helped blaze a trail for women in law.

Like Supreme Court Justices Sandra Day O'Connor and Ruth Bader Ginsburg, she became a lawyer in the days when few women practiced law. President Jimmy Carter appointed her to a seat on the federal bench in 1979.

She was born Dolores Korman in Philadelphia in 1932, the only child of Jewish immigrants from Poland. Her mother wanted her to be a teacher. But Dolores had other plans for herself. She applied to law school at the University of Pennsylvania and got in, becoming one of the female pioneers. Upon graduating from law school in 1956, she found few opportunities available for women lawyers.

"My story is the same as the stories we have all heard publicly now from Ruth Ginsburg and Sandra Day O'Connor," she said in an interview for a University of Pennsylvania oral history project. "We all had the same experience of knocking on doors and being told, 'We're sorry, we really have nothing for you. Would you like to be our librarian? Would you like to be a secretary? Would you like to write briefs in the back room?'"

At first, Sloviter thought that opportunities for women would open up once people saw lawyers like herself in practice. Then, in 1972, when she joined the law faculty at Temple University, she learned from her female students that not much had changed. They were having the same problems getting jobs that she had in the 1950s.

She decided it was time for action. Sloviter called for changes such as requiring law firms that recruited on

JUDGE DOLORES K. SLOVITER FOUND THAT IT WAS EXTREMELY DIFFICULT FOR A WOMAN—AND A JEWISH WOMAN AT THAT—TO GET A JOB AS A LAWYER WHEN SHE GRADUATED FROM LAW SCHOOL IN 1956. SHE LATER FOUGHT FOR EQUAL HIRING PRACTICES.

campus to adopt equal hiring practices. "It takes a while for these things to get through, but we did it, and it was successful," she said.

the government challenged the plaintiffs' notion that the new law unfairly singled out computer communications by pointing out that the Supreme Court already had ruled that a law could single out a certain medium.

One day later, on February 15, 1996, Judge Buckwalter issued his decision. He granted the TRO for the "indecency" but not the "patently offensive" part of the statute, stating that he was not clear that the "indecent" and "patently offensive" clauses in the CDA were synonymous. He believed that the word "indecency" by itself was unconstitutionally vague.

The split decision left the ACLU in a quandary. In the hopes of persuading the government to hold off on enforcing the "indecent" clause of the act, the ACLU began meeting with lawyers for the Department of Justice. The government agreed to refrain from enforcing any part of the statute while the case was being tried. If the law were found constitutional, however, the government could begin prosecuting violations dating from February 8, 1996.

American Library Association and Online Companies

On February 25, 1996, a coalition that included the American Library Association (ALA) as well as online service providers America Online, CompuServe, Prodigy, and MSN, filed suit against the Department of Justice to overturn the CDA.

Other members of the coalition included the computer giants Microsoft and Apple, the American Society of Newspaper Editors, and a group of varied organizations called the Citizens' Internet Empowerment Coalition.

This suit, known as *ALA* v. *DOJ*, maintained that technological solutions, such as screening software, adequately protected children from offensive material, making laws such as the CDA unnecessary.

ALA v. DOJ was soon consolidated with ACLU v. Reno, but each coalition retained its own legal counsel. Prominent First Amendment lawyer Bruce Ennis headed up the legal efforts for the ALA coalition.

The two coalitions divided the work by handling different parts of the case. The ACLU focused on free speech while the ALA coalition concentrated on technological solutions and the infeasibility of the law's "good faith" defenses. Without a clear "safe harbor," adults would be reduced to what was "fit for children," which was clearly unconstitutional as a result of the landmark case of Butler v. Michigan.

As the consolidated suit awaited trial, law students across the country participated in protests against the CDA. Student organizers circulated petitions, gathering an estimated 7,500 signatures. Many students wore blue ribbons or plastered blue tape over their mouths to symbolize the silencing of free speech.

Hansen fielded inquiries from the media. He maintained that the nature of the Internet made "cyberzoning" technically and economically infeasible. Unlike a bookstore owner who could gauge a customer's age by sight, he said, the Internet offered no way to determine a user's age. "To comply with the law, you have to block your site to everyone," Hansen said.

Passions ran high on both sides of the case. Groups such as the National Center for Children and Families spoke in favor of the CDA. The Internet, they said, should be required to take steps similar to those of convenience stores that are required to keep pornographic magazines away from children.

GETTING READY FOR TRIAL
Lawyers for both sides got to work preparing their case for the hearings scheduled to begin on March 21, 1996. District

Judge Stewart Dalzell would join Judge Dolores Sloviter and Judge Walter Buckwalter on the three-judge panel.

ACLU LAWYER CHRIS HANSEN STANDS OUTSIDE THE PHILADELPHIA COURTROOM AFTER PRESENTING ARGUMENTS AGAINST THE COMMUNICATIONS DECENCY ACT ON MAY 10, 1996.

At ACLU headquarters in New York, Hansen found himself faced with one major challenge. He needed to call into question the legal precedent set by the "seven dirty words" case.

If the plaintiffs could show that the Internet was different from the broadcasting medium, they could build a case for overturning the CDA. Hansen familiarized himself with how the Internet worked and lined up expert sources who could show how the Internet differed from other media. Unlike radio or television, he discovered, the Internet required users to consciously choose material before it appeared. For Hansen, this meant that the Internet should be given the highest degree of First Amendment protection. The information superhighway lacked the elements of surprise and intrusiveness that justified government regulation of radio and television.

"My view is that you win a case on the facts," says Hansen, who was forty-nine years old in 1996. "By the time you get to court, the facts inevitably lead to the results you want."

Beeson brought her academic background in folklore to the case. She believed that the stories of "real people" would win the case for the plaintiffs. "You're not going to convince people by talking about abstract principles," she said. "They'll only get excited if you make it real."

To accomplish this, she worked closely with the plaintiffs on their affidavits. The process involved a fair amount of back and forth. She would begin by describing what should be included, then review a draft, noting which points needed to be clarified or fleshed out. She did little editing because she wanted each affidavit to tell the plaintiff's story in his or her own words.

Kiyoshi Kuromiya, director and founder of the Critical Path project, an AIDS prevention program, became one of the most-often quoted plaintiffs in the case. In his affidavit, he explained how AIDS information could be a matter of life and death.

"Critical Path does not intend to attempt to censor the information it provides," Kuromiya wrote in his affidavit. "In our view, to do so would be to condemn those who need the information to needless illness and death."

At the Department of Justice, Coppolino and his three colleagues reviewed the plaintiffs' affidavits and scheduled their depositions. During the depositions, the lawyers questioned the prospective witnesses to prepare for the trial. The lawyers divided up the depositions because there were so many to be handled. On one particularly busy day, each lawyer deposed a witness in a different conference room. During lunch, they compared notes on each deposition.

In keeping with the procedures laid out by the judges, testimony would be submitted by affidavit to save time. The testimony would last five days, with each side given time to present and cross-examine witnesses. First, though, both sides would need to wire the courtroom for the Cybertrial of the Century.

FIVE
THE LOWER COURT

ON MARCH 21, 1996, THE THREE JUDGES took their places behind computer terminals especially installed for the case of *ACLU* v. *Reno*. Spectators in the packed courtroom could watch the computer demonstrations on two large screens.

"Internet 101," one observer dubbed the proceedings.

On the first day of testimony, judges saw demonstrations of how screening software could block sites such as those posted by *Penthouse* and *Playboy* magazines. When Scott O. Bradner, a Harvard University computer consultant, took the witness stand, Judge Stewart Dalzell asked whether the Harvard College Library card catalogue could potentially receive an "adults only" rating. Yes, said Bradner. It would be too difficult to rate every one of the millions of references, so the whole catalogue might have to be placed off limits.

Plaintiffs Kiyoshi Kuromiya of Critical Path AIDS Project and Patricia Nell Warren of Wildcat Press and the YouthArts e-zine also testified. Kuromiya said he found the CDA unclear. "I don't know what 'indecent' means," he said. "I don't know what 'patently offensive' means in terms of providing life-saving information to people with AIDS, including teen-agers."

Warren, too, questioned the meaning of the terms

KIYOSHI KUROMIYA OF CRITICAL PATH AIDS PROJECT TESTIFIED ON THE PLAINTIFFS' SIDE.

"indecent" and "patently offensive." "What I'm concerned about is that certain people in this country will perceive the entire area of gay literature to be indecent or patently offensive," she told the judges.

On Day 2, computer expert Donna Hoffman of Vanderbilt University testified for the plaintiffs. Hoffman, who had criticized the *Time* article about cyberporn, believed that the Internet was different from the broadcast media because individuals made more conscious choices. "Individuals do not passively receive information, nor does the information suddenly appear, surprising them," Hoffman stated in her affidavit.

Jason Baron, a lawyer for the Department of Justice, set out to show that this was not always the case. Using the example of a student doing research on Louisa May Alcott's book *Little Women*, he punched in the keywords "little" and "women." The fifth entry on the list of results read, "See hot pictures of naked women!"

"Isn't it possible, Professor Hoffman, that a child might be surprised in stumbling across that entry in the context of an online search?" Baron asked in his cross-examination.

"It's possible," Hoffman said, adding that a more targeted search, such as one that included Alcott's name as well as "little women," would yield better results.

Judges Sloviter and Dalzell, however, pointed out that children inexperienced with the Internet might conduct such inexpert searches.

On April 1, the third day of hearings, a representative for America Online said the company would consider imposing a total or partial ban on popular services such as chat rooms if the CDA were to take effect. In addition, ACLU associate director Barry Steinhardt took the stand.

Steinhardt described a feature on the ACLU's Web site in which users were asked to guess the "seven dirty words" banned by the Federal Communications Commission. Said Steinhardt: "We cannot discuss important civil liberties issues that involve censorship without using the words that are being censored."

After three days of plaintiff testimony, the government put its two expert witnesses on the stand. On April 12, the government's first expert, Special Agent Howard A. Schmidt of the Air Force Office of Special Investigations, gave the court a live Internet tour and demonstration.

When asked by the judges how a safe-sex Web site illustrating how to put a condom on an erect penis would be affected by the law, Agent Schmidt said that because the context was "educational, not purely for pleasure purposes," he would not censor the site but advise the publishers to post warnings. Then Judge Dalzell asked how he would rate an online copy of the controversial *Vanity Fair* magazine cover featuring the actress Demi Moore nearly naked and eight months pregnant.

Agent Schmidt replied that, in that case, the CDA would apply because the image was "for fun." He also said that the community standard for offensiveness might be different for Minnesota than it would be for New York.

Then, on Monday, April 15, the government's second technical expert, Daniel Olsen Jr., chairman of the Computer Science Department at Brigham Young University in Provo, Utah, testified about the Internet rating scheme he had developed. Olsen's scheme called for content providers to label potentially objectionable material in the Internet address with the tag "-L18," for not less than 18. For example, the site www.cyberporn.com could be renamed www-L18.cyberporn.com to identify that the site was for adults only.

Lawyer Bruce Ennis, of the American Library Association, asked whether Olsen thought his tagging system should extend to the "seven dirty words."

Olsen said he did.

Ennis and Hansen, the lawyer for the American Civil Liberties Union, questioned the feasibility of Olsen's scheme. For one thing, they said, it required cooperation from other parts of the online community, such as Internet browsers. For another, it would have no effect on the vast amount of sexually explicit material produced overseas, estimated at about 40 percent of the total. Finally, it would pose an unfair burden on content providers, the lawyers said.

The cross-examination of Olsen brought the five days of testimony to a close. The government's legal team took the Amtrak train back to Washington, D.C. By now, the porters recognized the government's legal team from all the trips back and forth between Washington, D.C., and Philadelphia—even saw them coming and held the train for them. Closing arguments were scheduled for Friday, May 10.

Coppolino looked forward to closing arguments as the most exciting part of the trial. He wanted to be so well prepared that he could rattle off answers without referring to his notes. He worked through Palm Sunday and Easter Sunday, and even had to skip the weddings of two friends.

Instead of traveling to Philadelphia the morning of closing arguments, he stayed over Thursday night at the Holiday Inn in Philadelphia. He worked late into the night, thinking of questions the judges might ask. Sometimes he spoke his responses aloud. Other times he jotted them down on a legal pad, keeping some answers, discarding others. He wanted his responses to sound like he was talking to a friend.

After a while, he put aside all his papers and cleared his head so he could be fresh in the morning. This was the biggest case of his career.

"When you're standing at the podium, you're like a

batter at the plate in the bottom of the ninth inning," he said.

CLOSING ARGUMENTS

On Friday morning, May 10, 1996, the lawyers and spectators crowded into the courtroom not far from the historic Liberty Bell in Philadelphia. At 9:32 a.m. the clerk convened the court. Everyone rose.

> Oyez, oyez, oyez, all manner of persons having any matter to present before the Honorable Dolores K. Sloviter, Chief Judge of the United States Court of Appeals for the Third Circuit, the Honorable Ronald L. Buckwalter and the Honorable Stewart Dalzell, Judges in the United States District Court for the Eastern District of Pennsylvania may at present appear and they shall be heard. God save the United States and this Honorable Court. Court is now in session, please be seated.

Judge Sloviter wished everyone a good morning and advised the lawyers to expect to be interrupted by the judges with frequent questions. Because of the questioning, the sessions were bound to run over the two hours given to each side, so no one should expect to hop on a plane that morning, she said. Then Judge Sloviter turned over the floor to the lawyers.

A CRIMINAL STATUTE

Christopher Hansen spoke first for the ACLU coalition. He began by talking about how the Communications Decency Act was a criminal rather than a regulatory statute, and so carried the penalties of fines, imprisonment, and a criminal record.

Next, Hansen turned to the rules of "vagueness" and

"overbreadth" for cases involving First Amendment and/or criminal statutes. The issue of vagueness, he said, affected far more people on the Internet than in broadcasting or other mediums. Unlike broadcasters like NBC or CBS that had their own staff attorneys, individuals who used the Internet would be put in the position of interpreting the phrases "indecent" and "patently offensive" on their own.

"Every single American may, as Mr. Olsen suggested, have to hire [his] own lawyer to determine what the precise contours of those phrases are," said Hansen.

Judge Sloviter asked him about the meanings of the two phrases. Did he think they were the same or different? "There are slightly different wrinkles," Hansen replied. ` Then Judge Dalzell asked how he could consider "patently offensive" vague when the Supreme Court, itself, had used the term.

Hansen replied that the *Pacifica* case dealt with the phrase only in the context of the George Carlin monologue. "We agree that it is legitimate for the FCC to regulate this monologue, to make it go at three in the morning instead of three in the afternoon," he said.

Furthermore, Hansen said, *Pacifica* contradicted the government's suggestion that the CDA targeted pornography. He found it hard to imagine anyone aroused by George Carlin's monologue.

Finally, he noted that the "seven dirty words" case took place in a regulatory and not a criminal context. If criminal penalties were in question, the Supreme Court might have reached a different decision.

Next, Hansen moved on to the question of "overbreadth." Citing the 1957 case of *Butler* v. *Michigan*, he argued that the CDA would reduce adults to reading only what was fit for children. Furthermore, the act would deprive minors, particularly teens, of valuable information such as how to protect themselves against AIDS and pregnancy.

"How do you answer the government's argument that the act couldn't possibly be read to apply to information of that sort?" Judge Sloviter asked.

Hansen replied that the law made no exemptions for material that lacked prurience or had serious value. "Well, if that's the case, it seems to me safer sex information is most certainly at jeopardy under this statute," he said.

Judge Dalzell responded with a hypothetical question. What if Senator Exon and Senator Coats gave him a pen to rewrite the law. What kind of law would he propose?

Hansen replied that the nature of the Internet made it difficult to regulate.

"So your position is then that you would give the pen back to Senator Exon and Senator Coats and just say I'm terribly sorry but for this medium we can't do it? Is that— is that your position?" Judge Dalzell asked.

"Well, yes," Hansen said, "but I have a better solution." Screening software, he said, would enable parents to protect their children without sacrificing anyone's constitutional rights.

Judge Dalzell asked how the government could make sure that happened.

"Relax for a second, it's happening," Hansen replied.

NO SAFE HARBOR

Next, Bruce Ennis spoke for the American Library Association coalition about the problems the statute's "safe harbor" defenses posed for noncommercial users. Ennis described the three categories of safe harbor defenses as "charging," "screening," and "warning."

The first category involved the use of credit cards. Ennis spoke about how Congress modeled the CDA on the dial-a-porn law.

"It thought the dial-a-porn analogy would work," he said. "It doesn't because the vast majority of the speakers on the Internet do not charge for access to their speech." Because credit card companies verified only commercial transactions, noncommercial sites would be unable to take advantage of the first "safe harbor" defense.

Ennis moved on to the second defense—screening. This defense, he said, was impossible under the current technology.

The third defense—warning or "tagging"—also posed technological problems. Because much of pornography came from abroad, the government's L18 tagging scheme would be less effective in blocking sexually explicit material than the online servers' own parental controls, Ennis argued. Indeed, he said, the CDA did little, if anything, to protect children from inappropriate speech that would not already be done as a result of market forces and screening software.

Ennis finished off his closing arguments by addressing the difference between the Internet and broadcast television or radio.

"You don't turn on your computer and sexually explicit images pop on your screen," he said, "You turn on your computer and you have to select where you want to go to get there."

Judge Dalzell brought the session to a close by asking Ennis the same hypothetical question as Hansen. "Senator Exon and Senator Coats give you the pen to write . . . , do you give it back to them, or do you write something?" he asked.

Ennis echoed Hansen's sentiments. "Let the market work for a while and see if you even need any governmental intervention of this nature whatsoever."

But, Ennis continued, if he were pushed to come up with a different law, he would find ways to make it more narrowly tailored. For instance, he might try to regulate advertising of the so-called teaser ads for porn sites since advertising was judged by a less strict standard of scrutiny than noncommercial speech.

He also suggested taking out the phrase about "available to minors," which essentially banned all speech, and simply requiring fair warning for patently offensive material. Still, he doubted such a scheme would pass constitutional muster.

Judge Sloviter responded with typical candor to the possibility of another court challenge. "It doesn't help to suggest what you think is unconstitutional now, does it?" she asked, eliciting laughter from the crowd.

Ennis replied, "I was just trying to respond to Judge Dalzell's question."

Judge Dalzell brought the session to a close by noting that he would not want to repeat the kind of constitutional challenge to dial-a-porn that involved ten years of litigation.

GOVERNMENT ARGUMENTS

After a recess from 11:07 a.m. to 11:28 a.m., lawyers for the Department of Justice made their closing arguments. Anthony Coppolino spoke first. Facing the three federal judges, Coppolino felt a surge of adrenaline.

As soon as Coppolino finished his introductions, Judge Sloviter launched into a series of questions. First she wanted to know if Coppolino thought the provisions for "patently offensive" and "indecent" were one and the same.

"Yes, I do, your Honor," Coppolino replied.

"So you want us to write into [clause] A the words describing sexual or excretory activities or organs?" Judge Sloviter asked.

"Well, yes, your Honor," Coppolino replied.

Next, Judge Sloviter asked what types of material the statute covered.

Coppolino said that the indecency standard encompassed only pornography and shocking, offensive, or vulgar speech such as George Carlin's monologue. Unlike his expert witness, Dan Olsen, he did not believe that people could be held liable for violating the statute every time they used a swear word.

"Our point," Coppolino said, "Is that it's not simply anything about sex or anything with an expletive, the parameters are fairly specific."

Judge Dalzell wanted more details. "Let's put some flesh on it because . . . I share Judge Sloviter's befuddlement on this point," he said.

Judge Sloviter said that she was not sure she would use the term "befuddlement" to describe her state of mind.

"Well, all right, then I will describe it for myself as that," Judge Dalzell remarked.

Once again, laughter filled the courtroom. Judge Dalzell expressed his concern about how individual prosecutors might interpret the indecency standard.

Coppolino acknowledged the judge's concerns. "Your Honor, I think that we cannot provide assurance that there might not be a prosecutor that's going to take the most absurd case or very extreme case." he said.

After Coppolino reiterated his belief that the statute would affect only a narrow array of speech, Judge Dalzell reminded him that Congress had specifically rejected the variable obscenity standard for the broader parameters of indecency.

"How could we engraft a harmful to minors test when Congress specifically rejected it?" Judge Dalzell asked.

Coppolino replied that Congress already had established parameters for indecency under the "dial-a-porn" law. But, Judge Dalzell pointed out, none of the plaintiffs in *ACLU* v. *Reno* dealt in pornography.

Coppolino agreed. "In our view not one of them falls within the legitimate sweep of this statute."

The judges wondered how the community standards of indecency could be applied to a global medium like the Internet. Coppolino reiterated his belief that the indecency standard applied to a narrow range of speech.

Judge Sloviter said she was still unclear about whether or not the indecency standard applied to works of value such as *Angels in America*, a Broadway play about AIDS. Coppolino replied that it depended on the context. The work as a whole would not be considered indecent, but excerpts taken out of context might be.

"But wouldn't that cover almost all the plays on Broadway today?" Judge Sloviter asked.

"No, I would say not, your Honor," Coppolino replied.

Next the judges raised the question of whether the Internet was more like broadcasting or the print medium. Coppolino answered that it was more like broadcasting because of its elements of pervasiveness and surprise.

NEWSPAPER DECENCY ACT

Judge Dalzell spoke about how his ten-year-old son liked reading the sports section of the newspaper. Once, while looking for the sports, he came upon a graphic photo of a Liberian prisoner being shot to death. He asked whether Congress should pass a Newspaper Decency Act requiring newspapers to put any depiction of murder below the fold.

Coppolino's mind flashed to a memory of himself as a ten-year-old looking for the baseball scores in 1968 and discovering that Robert F. Kennedy had been assassinated. No, he told Judge Dalzell, he would not want to restrict the depiction of serious and tragic news events.

INQUIRY RAISES QUESTIONS

In the middle of the *ACLU* v. *Reno* trial in Philadelphia, a news story sent shock waves through the courtroom.

Newspapers reported that a letter from a conservative Christian group had set off a Federal Bureau of Investigations (FBI) inquiry of CompuServe, one of the plaintiffs in the case, for possible violations of the CDA. Why had the Department of Justice launched such an inquiry while the court case was pending?

During closing arguments on May 10, Judge Stewart Dalzell pointedly questioned defense attorney Jason Baron about the CompuServe incident. Even though CompuServe posted warnings on its adult-oriented sites and provided free blocking software to users, the government's "safe harbor" defense had failed to protect the company from accusations of breaking the law.

Baron replied that the Justice Department had suspected obscenity violations independent of the CDA. Because obscenity was against the law, the government was justified in its inquiry, he said.

But, after viewing the exhibits, Judge Dalzell found nothing to justify such suspicions. On May 15, he issued an order prohibiting the government from initiating any other reviews of online publishers unless child pornography or obscenity was suspected.

The CDA, he said, dealt only with material with "sexual" or "excretory" content. The print equivalent would be pornographic magazines, which were already off-limits to minors like Judge Dalzell's son.

"He couldn't go into a drugstore and buy *Penthouse* or *Playboy*," Coppolino said. "They can't sell that to minors. He couldn't go into an adult bookstore, he couldn't go into an adult movie theater, and he can't get that stuff."

Next Judge Dalzell raised the question of how chat rooms would be regulated. Should Congress be able to regulate conversations on the Internet that resembled those on the telephone?

Coppolino pointed to dial-a-porn. Some types of phone conversations could be regulated.

"But dial-a-porn doesn't go beyond porn, by definition," Judge Dalzell replied.

"Your Honor, that's right," Coppolino replied. "But we're kind of back now to does this indecency standard cover every time someone uses a dirty word in a chatroom when they get mad. And I would suggest that that's really not what it's intended to cover."

Coppolino closed his arguments by describing the inadequacy of screening software. At 12:46 p.m., the court recessed for lunch.

"SAFE HARBOR DEFENSES"

After lunch, Department of Justice lawyer Jason Baron began presenting the second part of the government's case. Once again, the three judges frequently interrupted with questions.

Judge Buckwalter wanted to know about the feasibility of the "safe harbor" defenses. Baron answered that "tagging" was the simplest solution.

"That's not available now," Judge Buckwalter said. "That's not available now, and it's —"

President Bill Clinton holds up a V-chip at the Library of Congress on February 8, 1996, where he signed the Communications Decency Act into law. The V-chip allows parents to stop their children from watching television shows that they feel are inappropriate.

THE LONE PLAINTIFF

Joe Shea filed his own lawsuit against the Communications Decency Act (CDA) instead of participating in the American Civil Liberty Union's case.

"I was angry that the ACLU did not sign on to our case, as we were the first to announce," explained Shea, editor and publisher of the electronic newspaper *The American Reporter*. Shea announced his plans to challenge the CDA while it was still winding its way through Congress.

On February 8, 1996, the day President Bill Clinton signed the CDA into law, Shea published an editorial laced with obscenities as an act of civil disobedience against the new regulations. In a nod to history, the law firm that represented Pacifica in the "seven dirty words" case offered to represent Shea on a *pro bono* basis.

Shea filed his suit, *Shea* v. *Reno*, in New York federal court. Although it overlapped with *ACLU* v. *Reno*, Shea's case focused specifically on freedom of the press as opposed to the broader category of free speech. Shea believed that online publications like *The American Reporter* should have the same rights as print publications.

On July 29, 1996, a panel of three judges in New York federal court ruled in Shea's favor, reinforcing the Philadelphia court's decision in *ACLU* v. *Reno*. By the time *ACLU* v. *Reno* reached the Supreme Court, six federal judges had declared the CDA unconstitutional.

"It's hypothetical," Judge Sloviter said, finishing his sentence.

Baron replied that the technology already existed. "It's just a question of, as Dr. Olsen said, four hours of tweaking a Netscape proxy server to have 80 percent of the market put into place," he said.

Once such a system took effect, violations would be subject to criminal penalties. Judge Dalzell raised the question of plaintiffs like AIDS-prevention activist Kiyoshi Kuromiya, who wanted teens to be able to access his site.

"So it's better for Mr. Kuromiya to bear the risk of going to a Federal correctional institution?" Judge Dalzell asked.

"Your Honor," Baron replied, "I just will not concede that Mr. Kuromiya is within the scope of the act for the purpose of this discussion. And, if he doesn't want to avail himself of any access measures, well, then—then he can take the consequences."

Judge Dalzell turned to the question of screening software. He wondered if the CDA was needed "because parents like me . . . are worried about their ten-year-olds and twelve-year-olds and America Online and CompuServe and all those other folks better have an answer soon, or they're not going to have my business, or people like me."

Baron replied that such a solution was inadequate. "It's a flawed remedy, and there is a tremendous amount of inappropriate material that will seep through," he said.

After reiterating his belief in the feasibility of the "safe harbor" defenses, Baron drew his arguments to a close. "I have no further questions," he said before quickly correcting his slip of the tongue, "remarks to make, subject to your questions."

Judge Sloviter concluded the session by reminding the lawyers that no conclusions should be drawn from the

panel's pointed questioning. Then she called a five-
minute recess for Hansen and Ennis to confer on their
rebuttal arguments.

REBUTTAL ARGUMENTS
Both Hansen and Ennis used their rebuttal time to discuss
the constitutional problems with tagging. Requiring
speakers to label their own speech as a condition of speaking violated the constitution, they said. In addition, Ennis
pointed out that Congress already had rejected speaker
labeling of indecent material in broadcasting.

At the end of the rebuttal arguments, Judge Sloviter
thanked all the lawyers. A decision, she said, would be
issued in due course.

THE DECISION
Signaling a new era, the decision of the three-judge panel
arrived via computer. On June 11, 1996, the legal staff of
the ACLU crowded into Chris Hansen's office as the decision appeared on the screen.

In a unanimous decision celebrating the democratic
nature of the Internet, the three judges declared the
Communications Decency Act unconstitutional. All three
judges found the statute unconstitutionally broad. The
ACLU marked the event in an e-mail to members titled,
"Victory!"

Perhaps in the interest of saving time, the judges
wrote three separate opinions rather than trying to meld
their three voices into one. The opinions overlapped, but
each judge wrote eloquently about how he or she viewed
the case.

In her decision, Judge Sloviter questioned the government's need to protect older teenagers from material
considered indecent under the law. She pointed to *Angels
in America*, an award-winning play about AIDS, and news

reports about female genital mutilation as examples of work teachers might assign to eleventh or twelfth graders.

Judge Sloviter also questioned the government's argument that the law would cover only smut, not works of literature. "That would require a broad trust indeed from a generation of judges not far removed from the attacks on James Joyce's *Ulysses* as obscene," she wrote.

In addition, she took issue with the government's arguments about new technology. "I can imagine few arguments less likely to persuade a court to uphold a criminal statute than one that depends on future technology to . . . the reach of the statute within constitutional bounds," she wrote.

Even if "tagging" were available, she argued, requiring speakers to tag their speech would be "a burden one should not have to bear in order to transmit information protected under the Constitution." Moreover, she found the statute to be overly "vague."

Judge Buckwalter took a special interest in the question of "vagueness." Because the CDA lacked the clarity needed to inform persons as to what speech was criminal, he believed it violated the Fifth Amendment's "due process" clause. "Such unfettered discretion to prosecutors . . . is precisely what due process does not allow," he wrote.

Judge Dalzell, in turn, wrote eloquently about the possibilities of the Internet as a new form of communication. Praising the Internet as a forum where "dialogue occurs between aspiring artists, or French cooks, or dog lovers or fly fishermen," he wrote, "It is no exaggeration to conclude that the Internet has achieved, and continues to achieve, the most participatory marketplace of mass speech that this country—and indeed the world—has yet seen."

As Judge Dalzell saw it, the CDA would destroy the

democratic nature of the Internet by allowing commercial sites to flourish while noncommercial sites folded because of their inability to afford age verification. He argued that the Internet deserved the strictest First Amendment protection. Any government regulation of protected speech in cyberspace "could burn the global village to roast the pig," he wrote.

Both sides reacted quickly to the decision. While civil libertarians hailed the decision as a resounding victory for freedom of speech, supporters of the CDA criticized it as out of step with popular sentiment. The government appealed the lower court's decision to the Supreme Court.

Senator James Exon blasted the Philadelphia decision for brushing aside previous rulings upholding the indecency standard. "I am hopeful that the U.S. Supreme Court, relying on its own precedents, will find the CDA to be constitutional," he said.

SIX
SUPREME COURT ARGUMENTS

THE NEXT AND FINAL STOP for the case would be the Supreme Court.

With its majestic marble pillars and rich velvet curtains, the Court has long evoked an air of dignity, formality, and tradition. Quill pens adorn the four counsel tables. The nine justices still wear the kind of robes Abraham Lincoln once said made them look like long-winged black ants. They have ruled on the most pressing issues of the day. School desegregation. Abortion. And, now, free speech on the Internet.

Over the years, some lawyers have fainted before the Court, given the momentousness of their task. Others have deferred to their more senior colleagues.

But both Chris Hansen of the American Civil Liberties Union (ACLU) and Bruce Ennis of the American Library Association coalition welcomed the opportunity to appear before the nation's highest court. The two lawyers hoped to share oral arguments in Washington, D.C., much as they had in Philadelphia. However, the Supreme Court denied their request. Only one lawyer from both coalitions would be allowed to appear.

But who would that be—Hansen or Ennis? To decide, the two groups held a moot court before three judges. Two out of the three judges chose Ennis. A disappointed Hansen accepted the verdict. (In a moot court, law students usually

BRUCE ENNIS (RIGHT), THE LAWYER REPRESENTING THE AMERICAN LIBRARY ASSOCIATION COALITION IN THE PHILADELPHIA LAWSUIT, WAS CHOSEN TO PRESENT THE ACLU'S CASE IN FRONT OF THE SUPREME COURT.

receive a problem ahead of time, and then research and prepare the case as if they were lawyers. Typically, participants write briefs and prepare oral arguments.)

"It was awful," Ann Beeson recalled. "We were all friends and colleagues. But we thought it was our case."

A new Supreme Court ruling also raised concerns. In *Denver Area Telecommunications Consortium* v. *FCC*, a plurality of the Court rejected a vagueness challenge to the indecency standard for cable television. The Court's decision made no mention of the ACLU's recent victory in Philadelphia.

At ACLU headquarters in New York, Chris Hansen knew that one victory did not ensure another. The Supreme Court more often than not reversed lower-court decisions. Over the years, Hansen had found the nine justices hard to predict. Even though he knew their general leanings on questions involving civil liberties, they sometimes surprised him.

Just before oral arguments, he predicted that the justices would steer clear of technical matters. A question by Justice Sandra Day O'Connor proved him wrong—again.

"I try not to predict," he said. "I get it wrong too much."

support for the government

On the other side of the case, a number of organizations headed by the anti-pornography group Enough Is Enough filed a friend of the court brief in support of the Communications Decency Act (CDA). They wrote that in a more innocent time the Court had ruled so adults would not be reduced to what was "fit for children." Now, children were at risk of reading only what was "fit for adults."

Taking issue with the lower court's decision, they argued that it was possible to establish a system of age verification on the Internet. Such a system was needed, they

Donna Rice Hughes (left), once best known for sitting on the lap of presidential candidate Gary Hart, later became president of Enough is Enough, a parents' group against pornography.

said, because pornography harmed children. The habitual use of "soft" pornography, for instance, sometimes created a desire for more deviant, violent pornography.

"Few parents, no matter how liberal their political views, want their children exposed to some of the material that's the fringes of the Internet," they wrote.

government's brief

Meanwhile, in Washington, D.C., attorneys for the government went to work on preparing their brief. This time the case would be in the hands of the solicitor general. The special office of the solicitor general, within the Department of Justice, represents the United States government in cases before the Supreme Court. Dubbed the "tenth justice," the solicitor general still wears a traditional nineteenth century style cutaway jacket with tails.

Deputy Solicitor General Seth Waxman would be representing the office. As a lawyer, Waxman had a reputation for being unflappable and a bit of a comedian. In one of his articles, he quoted Daniel Webster as saying a great lawyer "must first consent to be only a great drudge." Waxman believed that every argument demanded what others might describe as "overpreparation."

As *Reno* v. *ACLU* headed for the Supreme Court, the government's lawyers developed a new strategy. Instead of defending the CDA as a whole, they divided it into three separate parts in keeping with its different clauses.

> • the "transmission provision"—transmission of "indecent" material knowing that the recipient is under the age of eighteen.
> • the "specific child provision"—knowingly sending "patently offensive" material directly to a specific person or persons under the age of eighteen.
> • the "display provision"—knowingly using a computer service to display "patently offensive" material in a manner available to a person under eighteen years of age.

The lawyers criticized the lower court for invalidating the law in its entirety, arguing that each provision could be severed from the rest of the statute. Then they compared the provisions to three prior cases restricting free speech:

> • *Ginsberg* v. *New York* (1969)—prohibiting the sale of "girlie" magazines to minors.
> • *FCC* v. *Pacifica* (1978)—the "seven dirty words" case upholding restrictions on the airing of "indecent" broadcasts.
> • *Renton* v. *Playtime Theatres* (1986)—allowing zoning restrictions to keep adult movie theaters away from residential areas.

The "transmission" and "specific child provisions," they argued, were similar to laws against selling "girlie" magazines to children. Like *Ginsberg*, both clauses required the initiator of the "indecent" material to know the recipient was a minor.

Next, they turned to the broader "display provision." While acknowledging the display provision's possible impact on adult-to-adult communication, they noted that it, too, was constitutional in light of *Pacifica* and *Renton*.

"Just as it was constitutional for the FCC to channel indecent broadcasts to times of the day when children most likely would not be exposed to them, so Congress could channel indecent communications to places on the Internet where children are unlikely to obtain them," they wrote. "In effect the display provision operates as an adult 'cyberzoning' restriction, very much like the adult theater zoning ordinances upheld in *Renton* and *Young*."

"ELEVENTH HOUR EFFORT"

The ACLU's brief scoffed at the government's argument as an "eleventh hour effort" to salvage the CDA. Lawyers for the ACLU pointed to the differences between the CDA and the three previous cases. Unlike *Ginsberg*'s variable obscenity standard, the "indecency" law failed to exempt works of serious value or those lacking prurience. And, unlike *Pacifica*, which involved the more invasive medium of broadcasting, or *Renton*, which dealt with zoning, the CDA carried criminal, rather than civil, penalties, they wrote.

The ACLU's lawyers also took issue with the question of severability. Calling the severability argument a "smokescreen" to hide the unconstitutionality of the law, they argued that the act's defenses applied to all three clauses, showing that Congress had intended it to be taken as a whole.

They also maintained that, because the vast majority of Internet speakers could not distinguish between minors and adults in their audience, the CDA would force adults to speak in language suitable for children. They reiterated their original argument that the act was unconstitutionally vague and overbroad.

Pointing to "vagueness," they argued that the government, itself, had caused confusion over what the law would cover, with its own expert witness, Dan Olsen, testifying that the act would apply to the use of each of the "seven dirty words." In terms of "overbreadth," the ACLU mentioned the act's impact not only on adults but also on minors, particularly older teens. One quarter of all new HIV infections in the United States involved young people thirteen to twenty. For plaintiffs like Kiyoshi Kuromiya, the future of free speech on the Internet depended on the Supreme Court.

ORAL ARGUMENTS

On the morning of March 19, 1997, a cold, freezing rain fell on the nation's capital. Outside the gleaming white Supreme Court Building, activists on both sides of the case held banners and signs.

The line snaked around the courthouse steps. Some, unable to get seats in the courtroom, stayed outside to talk to reporters.

Although the Court usually limited oral arguments to thirty minutes per side, *Reno* v. *ACLU* would allow an extra five minutes for each of the lawyers. The lawyers entered through the back door well ahead of the scheduled 10 a.m. hearing. In keeping with a longstanding tradition to show harmony of purpose, the judges all shook hands before the proceedings.

Promptly at 10 a.m., the marshal announced, "The Honorable, the Chief Justice, and the Associate Justices of the Supreme Court of the United States!" As the justices stepped from behind velvet curtains and took their places, everyone rose. Tradition called for the Chief Justice to sit in the middle, with the other justices sitting on alternate sides in order of seniority.

The marshal chanted the order for silence, "Oyez! Oyez! Oyez!" from the days when Anglo-Norman was the language of the English courts. It means, "Hear Ye! Hear Ye! Hear Ye!"

"All persons having business before the Honorable, the Supreme Court of the United States, are admonished to draw near and give their attention, for the Court is now sitting. God save the United States and this Honorable Court!" the marshal spoke, then pounded the gavel. In hushed silence, everyone sat down.

searching for metaphors

Deputy Solicitor General Seth Waxman spoke first for the government.

"Thank you, Mr. Chief Justice, and may it please the court," he began.

Although Waxman credited the Internet with revolutionizing information technology, he also warned that it had given children online "a free pass into the equivalent of every adult bookstore and video store in the country." The judges responded with a series of questions. Technical queries quickly gave way to inquiries of a more metaphorical nature.

Was the Internet like a library? A telephone? A public park?

Justice John Paul Stevens asked how a library would handle "indecent" catalogue items in cyberspace?

Waxman replied that it would put them in a separate area in cyberspace comparable to a different room in an actual library.

Then the justices compared the Internet to the telephone. Justice Stephen Breyer wondered how the CDA would affect high school students talking about their sexual experiences. "If you get seven high school students on a telephone call, I bet that same thing happens from time to time," he said.

Would a similar conversation on the Internet be considered a federal crime?

"There's no high school student exemption?" joked Justice Antonin Scalia, setting off a wave of laughter.

"Justice Scalia, you may find it in the legislative history, but it is not apparent on the face of the statute," Waxman quipped. Once again, laughter filled the courtroom.

Then Waxman brought the subject back to sex on the Internet. "My point . . . is that when the alternative is that every child in this country who has access to a computer and can click a mouse has access in his or her bedroom or home or library to *Hustler* magazine and *Penthouse* magazine . . . we think that this is a small price to pay, and Congress could legitimately say that this is a narrowly tailored alternative," he said.

Next, Justice Anthony Kennedy asked how the Internet compared to a public park. Waxman replied that he did not consider the Internet a public forum like a park or street corner. But, even if it were, he saw two situations that might apply. In the first, the government might require a theater company performing in a public park to screen for age. In the second, a person speaking with a bullhorn or in a loud voice on a park bench could be asked to move to a different place or use a cone of silence.

Justice Ruth Bader Ginsberg mentioned old laws that made it a felony to use offensive language in the presence of women and children. Wasn't the CDA based on a similar rationale?

No, Waxman replied. The old laws were unconstitutionally vague and restrictive to women as adults. Over the years, the Court has developed a clear standard for "patently offensive."

Next, the justices asked how the CDA would affect parents. Waxman replied that since Congress did not intend for parents to be held criminally liable for indecent material accessed by their children, the Court could add in an exemption for parents. Justice Ginsberg, however, questioned the Court's ability to alter the law as drafted.

Waxman stepped down after deciding to use the balance of his time for rebuttal. Chief Justice Rehnquist called on Bruce Ennis to make his argument for the appellees.

Appellees Argue Unconstitutionality

"Thank you, Mr. Chief Justice, and may it please the court," Ennis said, echoing the words Waxman had used earlier. Ennis then summarized the appellees' reasons for wanting the Court to find the CDA unconstitutional. Because the plaintiffs were responding to an appeal by the government, they were known as "appellees."

Once again, the justices turned to metaphor. Chief Justice Rehnquist compared the Internet to radio. In the early days of radio, he said, people might have argued, "the government shouldn't have to tell us we've got to have all this equipment." What was wrong with the government requiring people who wanted to use the Internet to make a similar outlay of expense?

"Chief Justice Rehnquist, there is an enormous difference between some burden, some cost, which the Court has upheld in other contexts—and a burden or cost that is economically prohibitive," Ennis replied.

Then the justices asked about new technologies to protect children online. Ennis noted that screening software could screen out pornography from abroad—material that would not be affected by the CDA.

Some of the justices wondered if the global nature of the Internet should deter efforts to uphold an American law. Justice Kennedy told Ennis that his concern about foreign pornography was not his "strongest argument."

Ennis agreed. "Our strongest argument, Justice Kennedy, is that this law will have the unconstitutional effect of banning indecent speech from adults in all of cyberspace," he said. "For 40 years, this Court has repeatedly and unanimously ruled that Government cannot constitutionally reduce the adult population to reading and viewing only what is appropriate for children."

Justice Kennedy, however, pointed to government's interest in protecting children. Didn't the government have a legitimate interest in protecting children who did not have adequate parental supervision?

Yes, Ennis replied, but the government could do so without depriving adults and minors of their First Amendment rights. Screening software, he said, offered the best solution because a child could be protected without a parent needing to be physically present.

"Mr. Ennis, if I had to be present whenever my sixteen-year-old is on the Internet, I would know less about this case than I know now," Justice Scalia remarked, prompting laughter from the crowd.

"That's the point, Justice Scalia," Ennis replied.

Ennis wrapped up his argument by maintaining that parental control devices on the Internet were more effective than those for broadcast television, cable, or telephone because parents did not need to be at home to monitor them. He sat down, and Waxman used his remaining time to defend the act.

Chief Justice Rehnquist thanked Waxman, as he had thanked Ennis. Then, with four words, the Chief Justice brought the proceedings to a close. "The case is submitted," he said.

SUPREME COURT JUSTICES

At the time of *Reno* v. *ACLU* in 1997, the Supreme Court consisted of Chief Justice William H. Rehnquist, Justice John Paul Stevens, Justice Sandra Day O'Connor, Justice Antonin Scalia, Justice Anthony Kennedy, Justice David Souter, Justice Clarence Thomas, Justice Ruth Bader Ginsburg, and Justice Stephen Breyer. Supreme Court Justices are nominated by the president and confirmed by the U.S. Senate.

CHIEF JUSTICE WILLIAM H. REHNQUIST

Nominated by: President Richard Nixon in 1971, confirmed 68 to 26 despite strong liberal opposition, served until death on September 3, 2005.

Viewpoint: Conservative, faulted by liberals for his perceived lack of concern for civil rights (wrote memo as law clerk for Justice Robert H. Jackson 1952–1953 in support of "separate but equal" doctrine for public schools and took stand in 1967 against integration plan for Phoenix schools as special Arizona state prosecutor); opposed abortion rights in landmark case of *Roe* v. *Wade* in 1973.

Background: Born October 1, 1924, in Milwaukee, Wisconsin, son of a newspaper salesman, grew up in suburban Shorewood; graduated Stanford University with both a bachelor of arts and a master of arts in political science in 1948; with a master's degree in government from Harvard University in 1950; graduated as valedictorian from Stanford Law School in 1952 (classmate of Sandra Day O'Connor), served as assistant attorney general for President Richard Nixon (1968–1971). Died September 3, 2005.

***Reno* v. *ACLU*:** Joined Sandra Day O'Connor in dissenting, in part, with the majority opinion.

JUSTICE JOHN PAUL STEVENS

Nominated by: President Gerald Ford in 1975, easily confirmed 98 to 0.

Viewpoint: Liberal but independent-minded, upheld the indecency standard for broadcasting in the "seven dirty words" case but not for the Internet in *Reno* v. *ACLU*.

Background: Born April 20, 1920, in Chicago, Illinois; graduated from Northwestern University Law School; rose to judicial prominence in 1969 as a member of a commission investigating whether two Illinois Supreme Court judges had taken a bribe, became a member of the U.S. Court of Appeals for Seventh Circuit in 1970.

***Reno* v. *ACLU*:** Wrote the majority opinion finding the entire Communications Decency Act unconstitutional.

JUSTICE SANDRA DAY O'CONNOR

Nominated by: President Ronald Reagan in 1981, confirmed unanimously, becoming the first female Supreme Court Justice; announced retirement in 2005.

Viewpoint: Moderate to conservative, regarded as "swing vote," often siding with conservative colleagues.

Background: Born March 26, 1930, on her family's cattle ranch in southeastern Arizona; first home had no electricity or running water; moved to El Paso, Texas, to live with her grandparents and attend a private school; graduated third in her class from Stanford University Law School in 1952, the same year as Chief Justice Rehnquist; became one of the first women to break into the predominantly male field of law; active in local Republican politics; married a fellow law student, raised three sons, and served as a state senator; appointed judge for the Arizona Court of Appeals.

***Reno* v. *ACLU*:** Dissented, in part, with the majority decision.

JUSTICE ANTONIN SCALIA

Nominated by: President Ronald Reagan in 1986, confirmed unanimously, becoming the first Italian-American Supreme Court Justice.

Viewpoint: Conservative; known for his sarcastic, witty, intellectually demanding and occasionally biting comments and questions during oral arguments; has opposed abortion rights, affirmative action, gay rights, and church-state separation; known by liberals as "the Terminator."

Background: Born March 11, 1936, in Trenton, New Jersey, the only child of an Italian immigrant father who taught Romance Languages at Brooklyn College and a schoolteacher mother; graduated valedictorian from Georgetown University in 1957; graduated *magna cum laude* from Harvard Law School in 1960; held positions in academia and government before being appointed in 1982 to U.S. Circuit Court of Appeals; established reputation as a leading conservative judge.

Reno **v.** *ACLU*: Voted with the majority to find the entire Communications Decency Act unconstitutional.

JUSTICE ANTHONY M. KENNEDY

Nominated by: President Ronald Reagan in 1988; easily approved after Senate rejected two previous nominees— Judge Robert Bork for his extremist conservative views and Judge Douglas Ginsburg for admitting he used marijuana as a student and a law professor.

Viewpoint: Moderate to conservative, a "swing vote" along with Justice Sandra Day O'Connor, has disappointed conservatives by upholding liberal precedents on abortion, flag burning, gay rights, and school prayer.

Background: Born July 3, 1936, in Sacramento, California; served as an altar boy, attended Stanford University like his mother and became a lawyer like his father; served on a commission to draft a tax-limitation initiative for then-Governor Ronald Reagan in early 1970s; appointed to U.S. Court of Appeals for the Ninth Circuit in 1975.

Reno v. *ACLU*: Voted with the majority to find the entire Communications Decency Act unconstitutional.

JUSTICE DAVID SOUTER

Nominated by: President George H. W. Bush in 1990, easily approved because of lack of views on controversial issues.

Viewpoint: Moderate to liberal; originally regarded as conservative but has resisted pressures from the political right to undo Court precedents of the 1960s and 1970s.

Background: Born September 17, 1939, in Melrose, Massachusetts; his father was an assistant bank manager, his mother worked in a gift shop; participated in legendary satirical theater group, the Hasty Pudding, as undergraduate at Harvard University; Rhodes scholar; graduated from Harvard Law School in 1966; served as attorney general for state of New Hampshire; judge on state's superior and supreme court.

Reno v. *ACLU*: Voted with the majority to find the entire Communications Decency Act unconstitutional.

JUSTICE CLARENCE THOMAS

Nominated by: George H. W. Bush in 1991; approved by a slim 52 to 48 margin after contentious confirmation hearings during which former employee Anita Hill accused him of sexual harassment; he denied the allegations.

Viewpoint: Conservative; has angered fellow African-Americans by opposing affirmative action and civil rights legislation; believes minority groups must succeed on their own merits.

Background: Born June 23, 1948, in Pin Point, Georgia; lived for first years of life in one-room shack with dirt floor and no plumbing; moved in with grandfather at age of seven; went to parochial school and planned to become a priest; received financial support to attend Yale Law School; felt snubbed by whites as affirmative action "token"; graduated from Yale Law School in 1974; became director in 1982 of United States Equal Employment Opportunity Commission (EEOC); appointed to Washington, D.C., Circuit of the United States Court of Appeals in 1990.

Reno v. *ACLU*: Voted with the majority to find the entire Communications Decency Act unconstitutional.

JUSTICE RUTH BADER GINSBURG

Nominated by: President Bill Clinton in 1993; quickly confirmed 97 to 3, becoming the second female on the Supreme Court and first Jewish member of the high court since 1969.

Viewpoint: Liberal but shares belief of many conservatives that courts should use judicial restraint; strongly backs gender equality, separation of church and state, and freedom of speech; known for her consensus-building, dispassionate, and well-reasoned arguments; viewed as liberal counterpart to her good friend, conservative Justice Antonin Scalia.

Background: Born March 15, 1933, to a comfortable middle-class family in Brooklyn, New York; graduated with high honors in government from Cornell University, distinguished herself academically at Harvard Law School, transferred to Columbia Law School when her husband took a job in New York; rejected for clerkship by Supreme Court Justice Felix Frankfurter in 1960 because of her gender; became first tenured female at Columbia Law School; successfully argued for women's rights before the Supreme Court, winning four out of five of her cases for the American Civil Liberties Union; appointed by

President Jimmy Carter as judge on United States Court of Appeals for the District of Columbia in 1980.

Reno v. *ACLU*: Voted with the majority to find the entire Communications Decency Act unconstitutional.

JUSTICE STEPHEN G. BREYER

Nominated by: President Bill Clinton in 1994; confirmed unanimously during a process that included so much praise for the nominee (an avid bird-watcher, bicycle rider, and gourmet cook) that National Public Radio commentator Nina Totenberg described the proceedings as "more of a coronation than an inquiry."

Viewpoint: Moderate liberal occupying the center of the court with Sandra Day O'Connor, David Souter, and Anthony Kennedy; disappointed liberals with his vote to uphold drug testing in public schools; upset conservatives with his support of affirmative action; described as showing his liberal credentials by supporting women's rights and press rights while establishing his conservative credentials by adopting a pro-prosecutorial approach in criminal cases.

Background: Born August 15, 1938, to Jewish family in San Francisco, California; received his law degree *magna cum laude* from Harvard in 1964; law clerk for Justice Arthur J. Goldberg, U.S. Supreme Court, 1964–1965, assistant special prosecutor for Watergate Special Prosecution Force 1973; chief counsel for Senate Judiciary Committee (1979–1981); professor of government, Harvard University (1978–1981), Judge in United States Court of Appeals for the First Circuit, Boston, 1981–1994 (chief justice 1990–1994).

Reno v. *ACLU*: Voted with the majority to find the entire Communications Decency Act unconstitutional.

seven
DECISION AND AFTERMATH

ON THURSDAY, JUNE 26, 1997, the Supreme Court declared the Communications Decency Act unconstitutional.

In a landmark 7 to 2 decision, the Court ruled that the Internet deserved the highest level of constitutional protection. Justice John Paul Stevens, who wrote the majority opinion, criticized the CDA for infringing on the free speech rights of adults in the name of protecting children. The statute, he wrote, "threatens to torch a large segment of the Internet community."

While Justice Stevens acknowledged the government's interest in protecting children from harmful materials, he found that the CDA lacked the precision the First Amendment requires for content-based restrictions on free speech. He also noted technological problems such as screening for age in many parts of cyberspace. In stirring language, he praised the speech-enhancing qualities of the Internet.

"Any person with a phone line can become a town crier with a voice that resonates farther than it could from any soapbox," he wrote.

Justice Stevens based his argument on both legal precedent and the nature of the Internet. First, he described how the CDA differed from the three decisions mentioned in the government's brief. Unlike *Ginsberg* v.

ASSOCIATE JUSTICE JOHN PAUL STEVENS, APPOINT-
ED BY PRESIDENT GERALD FORD IN 1975, WROTE
THE MAJORITY OPINION FINDING THE COMMUNI-
CATIONS DECENCY ACT UNCONSTITUTIONAL.

New York (the 1968 "girlie" magazine case), the CDA applied to noncommercial as well as commercial speech. A parent who e-mailed his or her seventeen-year-old freshman information about birth control, he wrote, could be accused of violating the statute.

Second, he pointed to the *Pacifica* decision, which he himself had written. While Pacifica channeled broadcasts such as the "seven dirty words" to nighttime hours, the CDA applied to all times of day. The Internet also was more accessible and less "invasive" than broadcasting, he wrote. He noted that users seldom encountered content accidentally.

Third, Justice Stevens addressed the question of "cyber-zoning." While *Renton* allowed zoning to keep adult theaters away from residential neighborhoods, it did not affect the content of those movie houses. The CDA applied to the content of speech itself, posing more First Amendment concerns.

In the next part of his argument, Justice Stevens criticized the CDA for being vague and overbroad. The CDA, he wrote, relied on only the "patently offensive" requirement rather than all three prongs of the Miller test for obscenity.

"Just because a definition including three limitations is not vague, it does not follow that one of those limitations, standing by itself, is not vague," Justice Stevens wrote. In a colorful footnote, he added, "Even though the word 'trunk,' standing alone, might refer to luggage, a swimming suit, the base of a tree, or the long nose of an animal, its meaning is clear when it is one prong of a three part description of a species of gray animal."

Justice Stevens harshly criticized the statute for its breadth. The terms "patently offensive" and "indecent," he noted, could apply to large amounts of non-pornographic material with serious educational or other value. He rejected the government's argument that two provisions of the act protected the rights of adults.

"The breadth of the CDA's coverage is wholly unprecedented," he wrote. "The regulated subject matter includes any of the seven 'dirty words' used in the Pacifica monologue, the use of which the government's expert acknowledged would constitute a felony. . . . It may also extend to discussions about prison rape or safe sexual practices, artistic images that include nude subjects, and arguably the card catalogue of the Carnegie Library."

PARTIAL DISSENT

Justice Sandra Day O'Connor and Chief Justice William Rehnquist agreed with most of the majority decision but disagreed in part. Writing separately for herself and Chief Justice Rehnquist, Justice O'Connor explained that she agreed with the majority decision in situations involving multiple speakers in cyberspace

"If a minor enters a chat room otherwise occupied by adults, the CDA effectively requires the adults in the room to stop using indecent speech," she wrote. "The CDA is therefore akin to a law that makes it a crime for a bookstore owner to sell pornographic magazines to anyone once a minor enters the store."

But she disagreed in cases involving only one adult speaker and a specific child. In those situations, she argued, the "indecency" or "patently offensive" provisions could be upheld.

REACTION
Within minutes of the decision, the ACLU hailed it as a resounding victory for free speech. "Supreme Court Rules: Cyberspace Will Be Free!" it declared in its press release.

Lawyer Chris Hansen took particular satisfaction in two facets of the decision. First, it united justices from across the spectrum. Second, it gave the Internet the same protection as books and newspapers.

For Beeson, the decision came as a complete surprise. "I was totally shocked by what a big win it was," she said. "I thought the best we could hope for was some kind of splintered decision."

BACK TO THE DRAWING BOARDS
On the other side of the case, supporters of the CDA vowed to continue their fight. Although the bill's original sponsor, Senator Jim Exon, had retired, his colleague, Senator Dan Coats, blasted the Supreme Court's decision as "out of touch with the American people." Coats and his supporters carefully studied the Supreme Court decision, then went back to the drawing boards to draft a new bill.

Senator Coats's new bill, the Child Online Protection Act (COPA), was drafted to address many of the Court's criticisms of its predecessor. Dubbed "the son of the CDA," COPA differed from the CDA in four important ways.

First, it substituted the narrower "harmful to minors" for the "indecency" standard. Second, it applied only to material on the World Wide Web and not to other services such as e-mail. Third, it applied only to commercial material. And, fourth, it changed the age requirement for minors from eighteen to seventeen years old.

Senator Dan Coats took up the fight that retired senator J. James Exon left behind. After the Supreme Court's decision, Senator Coats sponsored a new bill, the Child Online Protection Act.

The statute called for providers of sexually explicit material to establish credit card verification systems or other means to stop minors from entering their sites. The penalty for transmitting illegal material to minors was a jail term of up to six months, a $50,000 fine for each day of violation, or both. On October 21, 1998, President Clinton signed COPA into law.

Once again, a coalition led by the ACLU filed suit. The plaintiffs argued that the Justice Department itself had warned Congress that COPA would probably draw resources away from more important law enforcement efforts such as tracking down hard-core child pornographers. Plaintiffs included media organizations such as Time Inc. and *Salon* magazine, artists, booksellers, and free speech groups. Author and publisher Patricia Nell Warren, one of the plaintiffs in *Reno* v. *ACLU*, signed on to the new case, as did ACLU lawyer Ann Beeson.

"It is still unconstitutional," Beeson said about the new law, "and it still reduces the Internet to what is fit for a six-year-old."

Unlike *Reno* v. *ACLU*, the case to overturn COPA would be a long and circuitous one, involving two different presidential administrations. The plaintiffs began by asking for a preliminary injunction to prevent the new law from taking effect. On February 1, 1999, the district court granted their request. The court found that the plaintiffs were likely to succeed on their claim that COPA was unconstitutional for two reasons: first, because it imposed a burden on speech protected for adults, and second, because it was not the least restrictive means of protecting minors online. Filtering software, it said, presented a less restrictive alternative. The government appealed the decision to the Third Circuit Court of Appeals.

In reviewing COPA, the Court of Appeals asked a new

question: Could "community standards" be constitutionally applied to cyberspace? It answered no, that the community standard, in itself, rendered the statute unconstitutionally overbroad. Such a standard would unfairly give "the most puritan communities" an effective veto over a medium with no geographical borders.

The case of *Ashcroft* v. *ACLU* (now named for John Ashcroft, who was President Bush's attorney general at the time), moved up the next rung to the Supreme Court. On May 13, 2002, the Court decided that the community standards question did not, in itself, render the statute unconstitutional. Nevertheless, the Court kept the preliminary injunction in place and sent the statute back to the lower court for review.

The Court of Appeals once again found the statute unconstitutional. This time, the court held that the law did not meet the First Amendment's "least restrictive test." Once again, the government appealed to the Supreme Court.

BACK TO THE SUPREME COURT

On Tuesday, March 2, 2004, the Supreme Court heard oral arguments for the second time in *Ashcroft* v. *ACLU*. Solicitor General Theodore B. Olson represented the government. In his introductory remarks, General Olson described how he had typed the words "free porn" into a search engine and come up with 6,230,000 possible sites. He argued that filtering software was both underinclusive and overinclusive, making it an unsatisfactory alternative to COPA. Moreover, he said, minors could disable the filters without their parents' knowledge.

Beeson spoke next for the ACLU coalition. She said that her clients faced three possibilities: self-censor their work, put up screens that drive away users, or risk jail time for making material available to the general reading public. The district court, she said, had found filters at least as effective as COPA.

"In closing, I just want to say again that this Court has repeatedly held that the Government can't burn down the house to roast the pig, especially with so many other tools available to protect minors more effectively than this statute does," Beeson said. "The Government cannot send adults to jail for displaying speech in the name of protecting children."

Then General Olson made his final points. Congress, he

SOLICITOR GENERAL TED OLSON ARGUED THE GOVERNMENT'S CASE IN *ASHCROFT* v. *ACLU*.

said, had examined all the possible alternatives, including tagging and filtering, and settled on COPA as the best solution in keeping with the Court's findings.

"At the end of the day, it's important to emphasize this is a . . . challenge to a statute constructed according to this Court's guidance, according to this Court's decisions as to how to deal with a very serious national problem," he said.

Chief Justice Rehnquist thanked General Olson, then brought the session to a close by saying, "The case is submitted."

Three months later, on June 19, 2004, the Supreme Court issued its decision on the Child Online Protection Act. While upholding the preliminary injunction, the narrow 5 to 4 majority sent the case back to the lower court for a full trial. The Bush administration would have another chance to make its case.

INTERNET SAFETY ACTIVIST

When Donna Rice Hughes joined the fight against cyber-porn, many reporters already knew her name.

Nine years earlier, she had grabbed headlines in another sexually controversial matter. Donna Rice was the "other woman" in a 1987 scandal involving married presidential candidate Gary Hart.

Her transition from scandal participant to anti-pornography activist brought her back to her roots. Born into a conservative Baptist family, she recovered from the trauma of tabloid fame by falling back on her faith. In 1995, she reemerged as Donna Rice Hughes, Internet Safety Expert (she had married technology executive Jack Hughes a year earlier). It took a while for reporters to connect her to the Donna Rice of the scandal. When they did, a flurry of publicity followed. At least one reporter quipped, "Yes, *that* Donna Rice."

But she wasn't quite *that* Donna Rice. She now saw pornography in a different light—as possibly contributing to a date rape from her past.

At the age of twenty-two, Rice had lost her virginity to an older man against her will. For years, she blamed herself for the incident. Her life then took a series of "left turns." She fell in with a glittery crowd, dating both Prince Albert of Monaco and rocker Don Henley. Then she met Senator Gary Hart. A photo of him with the twenty-nine-year-old beauty aboard his yacht, the *Monkey Business*, sank his political ambitions and typecast her as a "bimbo" or "party girl."

To avoid recognition, she changed her hairstyle and even had her dentist make her special buckteeth dentures to alter her appearance. Gradually, she pulled her life back together.

In the winter of 1993–1994, a friend introduced her to Dee Jepsen, president of the anti-pornography group Enough Is Enough. Jepsen invited Rice to apply for a job. During the job interview, Rice asked what kind of harm pornography caused. Wasn't what people did in the privacy of their own homes their own business?

Jepsen told her that pornography's harms included promotion of the "rape myth"—that "no" meant "yes." Rice remembered hearing those words before. The older man who had forced her to have sex when she was twenty-two later told her he thought she was playing a game—that "no" meant "yes." She realized for the first time that she, too, might have been harmed by pornography.

Still, Rice worried about putting herself back in the public eye. "At first, I thought, 'This is not a good fit!'" she explains. "'The last things I want to get involved with are the media, politics, and sexually charged issues!'"

But she wanted some good to come from the scandal. "It's God's sense of humor to put you back on the horse that threw you," she says.

Alarmed by the graphic images she saw on the Internet, Donna Rice Hughes, as communications director of Enough Is Enough, made a presentation before Congress and the media showing downloaded images that Senator Exon later used in his famous "blue book." Her old foes, the media, became new friends, helping her get across her message about the dangers of the Internet. In 1998, she published her book, *Kids Online: Protecting Your Children in Cyberspace*.

Hughes's expertise won her a slot on the Child Online Protection Act (COPA) Commission appointed by Congress. She recommended, among other things, stiffer enforcement of obscenity laws. She takes issue with the ACLU's argument that COPA would affect works of value, such as art and literature, rather than just pornography.

"Look, we can't get bestiality prosecuted," she says with characteristic candor. "Are we going to be concerned about Michelangelo's David?"

Early on, Hughes developed a three-pronged strategy: educating the public, implementing new technologies, and stepping up law enforcement and public policy. She coined the catchphrase "Rules 'N Tools" to get across the message that parents should use a combination of household rules and software tools to keep their kids safe.

These days, she is working on a Rules 'N Tools initiative to raise public awareness about Internet safety. Over the years, she has seen steady progress in the development of Internet filters and the public's willingness to use them. However, on the legislative front, she feels stymied by the courts.

"We've seen what we predicted come true," she says. "Porn on the Internet is out of hand."

"When plaintiffs challenge a content-based speech restriction, the burden is on the Government to prove that the proposed alternative will not be as effective as the challenged statute," Justice Anthony M. Kennedy wrote in his majority opinion.

Justice Kennedy pointed to evidence showing that filters were not only less restrictive but also more effective than COPA. Unlike the federal statute, filters could block an estimated 40 percent of the pornographic material that comes from abroad. Moreover, a blue-ribbon commission created by Congress found filters more effective than adult identification or credit card verification in restricting minors' access to harmful materials.

Not all the justices, however, agreed with Justice Kennedy's opinion. Justice Antonin Scalia found COPA clearly constitutional. The three other dissenters, Justices Stephen G. Breyer and Sandra Day O'Connor and Chief Justice William H. Rehnquist maintained that the law should be interpreted to apply only to a narrow category of obscene material and should be upheld on that basis.

In his minority decision, Justice Breyer, joined by Justices O'Connor and Rehnquist, argued that COPA would not affect famous novels or serious discussions of sexuality. He also expressed skepticism about the effectiveness of filters, saying the software "lacks precision" and requires parents' willingness to pay for it, install it, and monitor their children's computer use.

But Justice Breyer was outvoted. As of 2005, COPA was still in legislative limbo.

LIBRARIES AND FILTERS

While COPA wound its way through the court system, Congress approved a new bill that dealt specifically with filters. The Children's Internet Protection Act (CIPA) designated federal technology funds for libraries that install filters on all computers. CIPA required use of the filters to block obscenity, child pornography, and material harmful to minors. On December 21, 2000, President Clinton signed CIPA into law.

The American Library Association and the American Civil Liberties Union filed suit to prevent CIPA from taking effect. The plaintiffs recommended "less restrictive means" such as privacy screens, enforcement of Internet use policies by library staff, and education and Internet training courses. Arguing that filters block out useful information as well as smut, they maintained that CIPA would censor constitutionally protected speech in order to suppress unprotected speech.

On May 31, 2002, a federal district court in Philadelphia agreed, striking down CIPA as unconstitutional. The government appealed the case to the Supreme Court.

As the case headed there, the Henry J. Kaiser Family Foundation released a new study showing that the problems of "overblocking" varied widely, depending on whether filters were set at the "least restrictive" or "most restrictive" settings. The researchers, who tested six commonly used filters, found that the filters blocked an average of just 1.4 percent of health sites at the less restrictive level but 24 percent of health sites at the most restrictive level.

On Wednesday, March 5, 2003, the Supreme Court heard oral arguments in the case of the *United States* v. *American Library Association*. Once again, Solicitor General Theodore B. Olson spoke for the government. He compared the libraries' decisions involving the Internet to those of selecting books or magazines for their collections. Libraries, he said, had traditionally refrained from carrying pornography.

Justice David Souter, however, pointed to the problem

of overblocking. What about the material that the library had not chosen to exclude?

General Olson said that libraries could make their own administrative decisions as well as disable the filters on request.

Next, Paul Smith, the lawyer for the respondents, faulted the law for inconveniencing and stigmatizing patrons who needed to ask the librarian to disable the filter. Smith brought his arguments to a close by pointing to "less restrictive" alternatives such as giving parents the option of asking for filters for their children.

Finally, General Olson spoke again, using his remaining time to bring the oral arguments to a close.

"What this statute does is gives the libraries the right, if they choose to accept Federal funds, to make the kind of decisions, to exclude pornography which there's no dispute in the record libraries have, from time immemorial, chosen not to put in their libraries," he said.

That June, the Supreme Court decided in General Olson's favor, reversing the lower court's ruling. Chief Justice William Rehnquist delivered the narrow plurality opinion, in which Justices O'Connor, Scalia, and Thomas joined, upholding the constitutionality of CIPA. The plurality opinion directly addressed the matter of "overblocking."

"Assuming that such erroneous blocking presents constitutional difficulties, any such concerns are dispelled by the ease with which patrons may have the filtering software disabled," Chief Justice Rehnquist wrote.

Justices Breyer and Kennedy joined in the plurality judgment but wrote their own opinions. Justices Stevens, Souter, and Ginsberg dissented from the judgment, agreeing with the lower court that CIPA was unconstitutional.

FLORIDA DEPARTMENT OF LAW ENFORCEMENT DETECTIVES HUNT INTERNET CHAT ROOMS FOR SEXUAL PREDATORS WHO VICTIMIZE CHILDREN.

CYBERPORN AND KIDS

How closely do the opinions of lawmakers reflect the sentiments of kids themselves?

To find out, Congress commissioned the Crimes Against Children Research Center (CCRC) at the University of New Hampshire to conduct a national survey of youth aged ten through seventeen who used the

Internet frequently. Chief researchers David Finkelhor, Kimberly J. Mitchell, and Janis Wolak released their results in a 2000 report, "Online Victimization: A Report on the Nation's Youth." Among their key findings:

- 25 percent of respondents were exposed to unwanted sexual material.
- 19 percent were sexually solicited online.
- 6 percent of the youth who experienced unwanted exposure to sexual material reported being very or extremely upset.
- 6 percent of respondents reported being harassed online.

The findings contradicted the Supreme Court's contention that users rarely encountered sexually explicit material by accident. They also provided a mixed view of cyberporn.

On the one hand, the researchers found that most respondents considered unwanted exposure to pornography little more than a nuisance—"litter on the information highway." On the other hand, about one quarter of those exposed said they were very or extremely upset by the exposure. And, while many other kids seemed unfazed by their own experiences with cyberporn, 74 percent said that adults should be very or extremely concerned about the problem of young people being exposed to sexual material on the Internet.

Finkelhor, Mitchell, and Wolak recommended looking into the types of online exposures most distressing to youth. "If we understood specifically what was distressing and harmful to even a minority of young people, policy might be crafted to minimize such conditions or provide education or even interventions that could prevent or minimize such reactions," they wrote.

free SPEECH ACTIVIST

Patricia Nell Warren champions free speech as if it's a matter of life and death. For her, it has been.

"Writing has been like a life jacket for me," says Warren, an author best known for her gay love story, *The Front Runner*. "That voice that talks to me has carried me through my darkest times."

As a plaintiff in both *Reno* v. *ACLU* and *Ashcroft* v. *ACLU*, Warren spoke about her concerns that gay subject matter would be censored. Her own books, she says, have been pulled from library shelves because of their positive portrayals of homosexuality. She knows from personal experience how damaging censorship can be for writers.

Born in 1936, Warren grew up on a ranch in Montana in a family that loved storytelling. Inspired by her family's tales, she wrote her early stories on a typewriter used to record the pedigrees of cows. Then her parents rewarded her with her own typewriter. After winning a fiction contest sponsored by the *Atlantic* magazine in college, she embarked on a career as an editor and writer.

In the late 1960s, Warren's job as an editor for *Reader's Digest* brought her to Spain, where heavy censorship had become a way of life. The fascist regime of Francisco Franco, she says, banned books and articles about controversial subjects such as homosexuality, women's rights, premarital sex, and birth control.

"Many people in the United States don't really understand what they're asking for," Warren says about censorship. "I got a good close-up look at what it meant for people. When you talk about censorship, it's something that permeates every crack and crevice of a culture."

After coming out of the closet as a lesbian, she published her 1974 breakthrough novel, *The Front Runner*. Several other novels followed. Then, in 1994, Warren got an invitation to speak at a special school for gay, lesbian, bisexual, and transgendered youth. The experience transformed her, prompting her to become a volunteer teacher at the school. She co-founded YouthArts, an e-zine for youth, after seeing how the Internet and the power of self-expression could transform the lives of teens.

"When it seemed like their families and schools were against them and that their lives were in pieces, something inside them was screaming to create," she says.

Worried that the Communications Decency Act could take that away, she became a plaintiff in *Reno* v. *ACLU* as well as *Ashcroft* v. *ACLU* and an ACLU suit against Internet regulation in the state of Arizona. YouthArts disbanded, but Warren launched a series of workshops for gay teens. By 2005, she had won a number of court cases but still felt unsettled. After 9/11, she says, people became more willing to justify censorship.

In Spain, she says, censorship started out as a political tool but spread to the entire culture. She worries that initiatives to curb pornography would be similarly applied to a wide array of topics. Looking ahead, she vows to continue her fight for free speech.

"I'm not against keeping sexual predators away from kids," she says. "The problem is when it's broadened so that someone who's seventeen can't buy a copy of my book."

Other reports followed. A Henry J. Kaiser Family Foundation study found that 70 percent of the nation's fifteen- to seventeen-year-olds had looked at Internet pornography, much of it graphically hard-core.

In 2004, *People* magazine published its feature story, "The Cyberporn Generation." As part of its research, *People* created a fictitious profile for Cr8zysue13, a thirteen-year-old girl said to live in New York and to like the music of Nine Inch Nails and Marilyn Manson. Then *People*'s undercover team went surfing to check out the response to their new profile. Cr8zysue13, it turns out, was propositioned in a "romance" chat room and deluged with racy junk e-mails and instant messages, many with links to more hard-core material.

People also interviewed former fans of cyberporn. One college student described how cyberporn had led him to mistreat women, believing he could toy with their bodies however he pleased.

HARASSMENT

Researchers also found that online harassment can be even more upsetting to youth than sexual solicitation or pornography. "The seamy side of the Internet is not all about sex, but includes plain old hostility, and maliciousness as well," Finkelhor, Mitchell, and Wolak wrote.

Harassment, they found, often involved people the kids knew. As a result, they did not feel protected by the distance or anonymity often associated with the Web. The harassment primarily took the form of instant messages (33 percent), chat-room exchanges (32 percent) and e-mails (19 percent).

Some examples:

• A seventeen-year-old girl said that people who were mad at her made a "hate page" about her.

• A fourteen-year-old girl said that kids at school posted a note from her boyfriend on the World Wide Web and sent it around as an e-mail.

• A twelve-year-old girl said someone posted a note about her on the World Wide Web that included swear words and involved sexual name calling.

In 2005, *People* magazine investigated the issue of cyberbullying in its article "The Web: The Bully's New Playground." The story described how a thirteen-year-old boy had committed suicide after being taunted by classmates in instant messages about his lack of size and prowess. His parents never knew about the problem until it was too late. *People* pointed to a new survey of teens online by MindOh!, an educational company, which found that nearly 80 percent said they had read or spread gossip online. More than half of the surveyed teens said they had seen Web sites that made fun of their peers.

Alongside the main feature, *People* offered some tips from experts for Internet safety. For instance, the experts say, victims of cyberbullying should print out copies of offensive messages, change their screen name, and notify a school official, the Internet server, and/or the police.

A COMPLEX MEDIUM

If any consensus has developed since *Reno* v. *ACLU*, it's that there are no simple solutions. The complexity of the Internet defies simple fixes.

"Though some might wish otherwise, no single approach—technical, legal, economic, or educational—will be sufficient," the National Research Council wrote in its 2002 report, *Youth, Pornography, and the Internet.* "Rather, an effective framework for protecting our children from inappropriate materials and experiences on the Internet will require a balanced composite of all these elements, and real progress will require forward movement on all of these fronts."

On the legislative front, Congress followed up COPA and CIPA with two more narrowly tailored bills. One penalizes sites that knowingly use misleading domains such as Whitehouse.com. The other established a Dot Kids domain as a safe environment for children. But, because of the competitive nature of the Internet, the Dot Kids domain has been slow to catch on.

Law enforcement officials, meanwhile, have focused their efforts on the illegal solicitation of minors and child pornography. In 2000, specialists estimated eight hundred cases, confirmed or under investigation, involving adults traveling to or luring youth they first "met" on the Internet. Specialized units from the FBI and local law-enforcement agencies have stepped up their presence online, often "decoying" themselves as youth to catch potential offenders.

Although researchers and public-policy experts applaud such efforts, they also recommend involving the general public in Internet safety. Internet protection, they say, can be taught much like safety education in the physical world. For instance, students can be taught when it's dangerous to give out personal information online.

Researchers also recommend that young people, themselves, be involved in public-policy decisions involving the Internet.

"Too much of the discussion about Internet safety to date has been between policy makers and parents, without consultation from young people themselves," wrote the authors of *Online Victimization*. "Policies crafted from such an adults-only discussion may be rejected, especially by older youth, because the policies may be seen as an effort to control rather than protect."

In the ten years since *Reno* v. *ACLU*, young people like Rheana Parrenas and Lea have become adults. Parrenas is currently working on a graduate degree in anthropology at Harvard University. She still writes, but the poetry of her YouthArts days has given way to opinion pieces for the *Lesbian News*. Although her editor has been supportive of her work, she continues to worry about censorship.

Lea, the ten-year-old shocked by a sexual comment in a child's chat room, has faded from public view. Her concerns, though, live on in the voices of other young people captured by researchers. For instance, a thirteen-year-old boy who loved wrestling got an e-mail with a subject heading that said it was about wrestling. The e-mail, however, contained pornography.

How can youth be protected from such unwanted communications without compromising the free speech rights of people like Rheana Parrenas? The debate begun during *Reno* v. *ACLU* continues, with no easy answers in sight. Laws and technology can only accomplish so much. The rest depends on people like you.

notes

INTRODUCTION

p. 7, par. 3, CNN, " The Case for the Communications Decency Act," http://www.cnn.com/US/970/3/cds.scotus/for/index. html

p. 7, par. 3–p. 8, par. 1, Voter Telecom Watch, June 14, 1995, "Exon-Leahy Debate," http://archive.cpsr.net/cpsr/nii/ cyber-rights/archive/Re-Legislation/Exon-Leahy-Debate

p. 8, par. 2, CNN, " The Case for the Communications Decency Act."

p. 9, par. 4, Opinion of the Court, *Ashcroft* v. *ACLU*, http://www. supremecourtus.gov

p. 9, par. 5, Stuart Biegel, "New Directions in Cyberspace Law," *Los Angeles Daily Journal* (May 23, 1996), http://www.gseis. ucla.edu/iclp/may96.html

p. 10, par. 1, Pamela Mendels, "Appeals Court Panel Gets Internet Primer in Court," *New York Times* (March 22, 1996). http://www.nytimes.com/library/cyber/week/0322 decency.html

p. 10, par. 4, Kathryn Kolbert with Kak Mettger, *Censoring the Web (Justice Talking from NPR)*, (New York: The New Press, 2001); Marjorie Heins. *Not in Front of the Children: Indecency, Censorship, and the Innocence of Youth* (New York: Hill and Wang, 2001). pp. 125–126.

p. 11, par. 1, Heins, *Not in Front of the Children*, p. 61.

CHAPTER ONE

p. 12, par. 3, Author's e-mail interview with Rheana Parrenas,

December 3, 2004.

p. 12, par. 6, Affidavit of Rheana Parrenas, http://archive.aclu. org/issues/cyber/trial/rheana.html

p. 14, par. 3, Author's phone interview with ACLU attorney Christopher Hansen (May 16, 2005).

p. 15, par. 1, Author's interview with Rheana Parrenas, December 3, 2004.

p. 15, par. 6, *Congressional Record*, Senate (March 7, 1996).

CHAPTER TWO

p. 17, par. 2, Marjorie Heins. *Not in Front of the Children: Indecency, Censorship, and the Innocence of Youth*. (New York: Hill and Wang, 2001), p. 23.

p. 17, par. 2, Nat Hentoff, *The First Freedom: The Tumultuous History of Free Speech in America*. (New York: Delacorte Press, 1980), p. 58.

p. 17, par. 3, Heins, *Not in Front of the Children*, p. 23.

p. 17, par. 4, Hentoff, *The First Freedom*, p. 283.

p. 19, par. 1, Holga G., and Edwin P. Hoyt. *Censorship in America* (New York: The Seabury Press, 1970), p. 15.

p. 19, par. 3, Kathryn Kolbert with Kak Mettger, *Censoring the Web (Justice Talking from NPR)* (New York: The New Press), 2001, p. 6.

p. 19, par. 4, Kolbert, *Censoring the Web*, p. 7; Heins, *Not in Front of the Children*, pp. 125–126.

p. 20, par. 3, Heins, *Not in Front of the Children*, p. 30.

p. 20, par. 4, Hoyt, *Censorship in America*, pp. 31–32.

p. 21, par. 3, Ibid., p. 28.

p. 22, par. 2, Heins, *Not in Front of the Children*, p. 61.

p. 22, par. 4, Hentoff, *The First Freedom*, pp. 285–286.

p. 23, par. 1, Heins, *Not in Front of the Children*, p. 64.

p. 23, par. 1, Judith Silver, "Movie Day at the Supreme Court or 'I Know It When I See It': A History of the Definition of Obscenity" http://library.findlaw.com/2003/May/15/132747. html

p. 23, par. 2, Hoyt, *Censorship in America*, p. 49.

p. 23, par. 4, Heins, *Not in Front of the Children*, p. 32.

p. 23, par. 5, Bob Woodward and Scott Armstrong. *The Brethren: Inside the Supreme Court* (New York: Simon and Schuster, 1979), p. 199.

p.23, par. 6, Woodward and Armstrong, *The Brethren*, p. 196.

p. 24, par. 1, Kolbert, *Censoring the Web*, p. 9.

p. 24, par. 2, Hentoff, *The First Freedom*, p. 292.

p. 24, par. 3, Heins, *Not in Front of the Children*, p. 86.

p. 25, par. 4, Ibid., p. 99.

GEORGE CARLIN'S MONOLOGUE

p. 26, par. 2, "Ten Questions For George Carlin," *Time* (March 29, 2004), p. 8.

p. 26, par. 51, "Filthy Words" (transcript), http://www.george carlin. com/dirty/dirty3.html

p. 26, par. 6, *FCC* v. *Pacifica Foundation* Decision, http://www. eff.org/ legal.cases/FCC_v_Pacifica/fcc_v_pacifica.decision

p. 27, par. 3, Kathleen Parker, "Access to Public Airwaves Gives Public Access to Exert Controls," *Los Angeles Business Journal* (March 29, 2004), p. 43.

p. 27, par. 4, George Carlin, "An Incomplete List of Impolite Words," http://www.georgecarlin.com

p. 28, par. 1, Ibid., p. 104.

p. 29, par. 1, George Carlin, *The Progressive* (July 2001).

p. 29, par. 2, *FCC* v. *Pacifica Foundation* Decision, http://www. eff.org/ legal/cases/FCC_v_Pacifica/fcc_v_pacifica.decision

p. 29, par. 3, Heins, *Not in Front of the Children*, p. 105.

p. 29, par. 4, Ibid., p. 104.

p. 29, par. 5, Greg Henderson, "Supreme Court Lets Stand Dial-a-Porn Restrictions (January 27, 1992) http://www/eff.org/ Censorship/Academic_edu?CAF/law/dial-information-vs-barr

p. 29, par. 6, Jonathan Wallace and Mark Mangan, *Sex, Laws, and Cyberspace* (New York: Henry Holt and Co., 1997), p. 218.

p. 30, par. 2, Heins, *Not in Front of the Children*, p. 125.

CHAPTER THREE

p. 31, par. 1, Voter Telecom Watch, June 14, 1995, "Exon-Leahy Debate," http://archive.cpsr.net/cpsr/nii/cyber-rights/archive/Re-Legislation/Exon-Leahy-Debate

p. 31, par. 4, The Exon Library, "Biography of Jim Exon," http://www.exonlibrary.com/biography.htm

p. 32, par. 3, Voter Telecom Watch, "Exon-Leahy Debate."

p. 32, par. 4, Harry Henderson, *Issues in the Information Age* (San Diego, CA: Lucent Books, 1999), p. 44.

p. 34, par. 1, "Patrick Leahy," *Biography Resource Center Online*, Gale Group (2001).

p. 34, par. 2, Jonathan Wallace and Mark Mangan, *Sex, Laws, and Cyberspace* (New York: Henry Holt, 1997), p. 180.

p. 34, par. 4, Voter Telecom Watch, "Exon-Leahy Debate."

p. 35, par. 1, Ibid.

p. 36, par. 2, Ibid.

p. 36, par. 5, Ibid.

p. 37, par. 1, Ibid.

p. 37, par. 3, Ibid.

p. 37, par. 6, Ibid.

p. 38, par. 2, Ibid.

p. 38, par. 4, *MacNeil/Lehrer News Hour*, transcript, (June 22, 1995), http://www.cdt.org/speech/cda/950622macneill_lehrer.html

p. 39, par. 1, Ibid.

p. 39, par. 2, Ibid.

p. 40, par. 1, Ibid.

p. 40, par. 2, Steven Levy, "A Bad Day in Cyberspace: The Senate Takes a Sledgehammer to Our Communications Future," *Newsweek* (June 26, 1995), p. 47.

p. 40, par. 3, Ibid.

p. 40, par. 4, Philip Elmer-DeWitt, "On a Screen Near You: Cyberporn—It's Popular, Pervasive and Surprisingly Perverse, According to the First Survey of Online Erotica. And There's No Way to Stamp it Out," *Time* (July 3, 1995), p. 38 (7).

p. 40, par. 5, Ibid.

p. 41, par. 1, Donna L. Hoffman and Thomas P. Novak, "A Detailed Critique of the TIME Article: 'On a Screen Near You: Cyberporn,'" http://elab.vanderbilt.edu/research/topics/cyberporn/time.dewitt.htm

p. 41, par. 2, Ibid.

p. 41, par. 3, Philip Elmer-De Witt, "Fire Storm on the Computer Nets: A New Study of Cyberporn, *Time* (July 24, 1995), p. 57.

p. 41, par. 4, Heins. *Not in Front of the Children: Indecency, Censorship, and the Innocence of Youth* (New York: Hill and Wang, 2001), p. 160.

p. 42, par. 1, Wallace and Mangan, Sex, Laws, and Cyberspace, p. 184.

p. 42, par. 3, *Congressional Quarterly Almanac,* 104th Congress (1995).

p. 42, par. 5, "Press Release on National Day of Protest from the Net," http://cdt.org/speech/cda/951213protest_pr.html

p. 43, par. 4, "Communications Decency Act of 1996," http://www. bigeye.com/cda.htm

THROUGH THE COURT SYSTEM

pp. 44–46, The Supreme Court Historical Society, http://www. supremecourthistory.org; Administrative Office of the U.S. Courts, http://www.uscourts.gov; Iowa Court Information System, http://www.judicial.state.ia.us/students/6
There is also a diagram on the last Web site.

p. 47, par. 3, Heins, *Not in Front of the Children*, p. 162.

CHAPTER FOUR

p. 48, par. 1, "Ribbon Campaigns," http://kwc.org/memory lane/ tjhsst/Fapage/rib.html

p. 48, par. 2, *Washington Post*, "The CDA: How We Got Here" (September 1997), http://www.washingtonpost.com/wp-srv/ tech/analysis/decency/background.htm

p. 48, par. 2, "A Quick Review of the Major Points of the

Responsible Speech Campaign," http://www.pageturners. com/ CDA/rs_pnts.htm

p. 48, par. 3, February 9, 1996, letter from Attorney General Janet Reno to the Honorable Albert Gore Jr., http://www. ciec.org/trial/abort_speech.html

THE MAGICIAN'S FEAT

pp. 50–51, *Computer Underground Digest*, (March 3, 1996); memo from ACLU lawyer Ann Beeson, http://venus.soci. niu.edu/~cudigest/CUDS8/cud819

p.52, par. 1–4, Author's interview with Anthony Coppolino, June 22, 2005.

p. 52, par. 6–p. 53, par. 2, "ACLU v. Reno Plaintiff's Brief Seeking a Temporary Restraining Order and Preliminary Injunction" (February 8, 1996). http://www.aclu.org/ Privacy/Privacy.cfm?ID=14101&c=252

p. 53, par. 3–4, "Defendant's Opposition to Plaintiffs' Motion for a Temporary Restraining Order," http://www.law. miami.edu/~froomkin/seminar/ACLU-Reno-TRO-Justice-brief.htm

p. 53, par. 6, Ibid.

DOLORES SLOVITER

pp. 54–55, "Dolores K. Sloviter Interview," www/law/upenn/ edu/bll/oralhistory/sloviter/sloviter_splash.htm

p. 56, par. 1, Ibid.

p. 56, par. 2, "Temporary Restraining Order in ACLU v. Reno, February 15, 1996," aclu.org/CriminalJustice/Criminal Justice. cfm?UD=14099&c=49

p. 56, par. 3, Peter Lewis, "Judge Blocks Law on Internet Smut," *New York Times* (February 16, 1996).

p. 57, par. 4, Pamela Mendels. "Law Students Protest Communications Decency Act," *New York Times*, March 15, 1996. http://www.nytimes.com/library/cyber/week/0315 protest.html

p. 57, par. 5–6, Pamela Mendels, "The Philadelphia Hearings: Free Speech v. Child Protection," *New York Times* (March 21, 1996), http://www.nytimes.com/library/cyber/week 1032decency.htm

p. 58, par. 4, Author's interview with Christopher Hansen, May 16, 2005.

p. 58, par. 5–p. 59, par. 1, Author's interview with Ann Beeson, May 31, 2005.

p. 59, par. 4, "Critical Path Affidavit in *ACLU et al.* v. *Reno*," http://www.aclu.org/Privacy/Privacy.cfm?ID=13943&c=252)

p. 59, par. 5, Author's Interview with Anthony Coppolino, June 22, 2005.

p. 59, par. 6, Stuart Biegel, "New Directions in Cyberspace Law," *Los Angeles Daily Journal* (May 23, 1996), http://www.gseis.ucla.edu/iclp/may96.html

CHAPTER FIVE

p. 60, par. 1–4, Pamela Mendels, "Appeals Court Panel Gets Internet Primer in Court," *New York Times* (March 22, 1996), http://www.nytimes.com/library/cyber/week/0322decency.html

p. 62, par. 1, "Free Speech Challenge to Internet Censorship Law," ACLU News Update (March 22), http://www.aclu.org/Privacy/Privacy

p. 62, par. 2, Pamela Mendels, "Day 2 in Federal Court: Smut on the Internet," *New York Times* (March 23, 1996).

p. 62, par. 3–6, "CDA Trial Transcript (March 22, 1996) http://www.epic.org/free_speech/censorship/lawsuit/transcript_3_22.1html

p. 62, par. 7, Pamela Mendels, "AOL May Abandon Chats if Decency Law Stands," *New York Times* (April 2, 1996), http://www.nytimes.com/library/cyber/week/0402decency. html

p. 62, par. 8–p. 63, par. 1, "Trial Update," Electronic Privacy Information Center (EPIC) (April 1, 1996), http://www.epic.org/free_speech/censorship/lawsuit/aclu_update_4_1.html

p. 63, par. 3–4, "ACLU v. Reno: Trial Update" (April 12, 1996), http://archive.aclu.org/news/n041296.html

p. 63, par. 5, Pamela Mendels, "Internet Ratings Systems Debated in Court," *New York Times* (April 16, 1996), http://www.nytimes.com/ library/cyber/week/0416decency.html

p. 64, par. 2, Testimony of Dr. Daniel Olsen (April 12, 1996), http://www.ciec.org/transcripts/April_12_Olsen.html

p. 64, par. 3, Mendels, "Internet Ratings Systems Debated in Court."

p. 64, par. 4–6, Author's interview with Anthony Coppolino, June 22, 2005.

p. 65, par. 1, Ibid.

p. 65, par. 3, *ACLU* v. *Reno*—Trial Transcripts, May 10 (closing arguments), http://www.epic.org/free_speech/cda/lawsuit

p. 66, par. 3, Ibid.

p. 66, par. 6, Ibid.

p. 67, par. 3–4, Ibid.

p. 67, par. 9, Ibid.

p. 67, par. 10, Ibid.

p. 68, par. 6, Ibid.

p. 69, par. 3, Ibid.

p. 69, par. 6, Author's interview with Anthony Coppolino.

p. 69, par. 8, *ACLU* v. *Reno* (closing arguments), http://www.epic.org/Freespeech/censorship/lawsuit/transcript_5.101.htm

p. 70, par. 4, Ibid.

p. 70, par. 9, Ibid.

p. 71, par. 6, Ibid.

p. 71, par. 8, Ibid.

p. 71, par. 9, Author's interview with Anthony Coppolino.

INQUIRY RAISES QUESTIONS

p. 72, par. 2–3, Pamela Mendels, "Prosecution of CompuServe Is Sought Under Decency Act," *New York Times* (April 11, 1996).

p. 72, par. 4, CDA Trial Transcript, http://www.epic.org/free_speech/cda/lawsuit/transcript

p. 72, par. 5, Pamela Mendels, "Judge Rebukes Justice Department for CompuServe 'Decency' Inquiry" (May 17, 1996), http://www.nytimes.com/library/cyber/week/0517 decency. html

p. 73, par. 2, *ACLU* v. *Reno* (closing arguments).

p. 73, par. 6, Ibid.

p. 73, par. 10, Ibid.

LONE PLAINTIFF

p. 75, Author's e-mail interview with Joe Shea, June 3, 2005.

p. 75, Peter H. Lewis, "Opponents of Indecency Rules on Internet Win Another Case," *New York Times* (July 30, 1996) p. A11.

p. 76, par. 5, Ibid.

p. 76, par. 7, Ibid.

p. 77, par. 3, Ibid.

p. 77, par. 5, ACLU, "Victory!" ACLU memo (June 26, 1996), archive.aclu.org/issues/cyber/trial/plamem.html

p. 77, par. 6, Pamela Mendels, "3 Judges. 3 Voices. 1 Conclusion." *New York Times* (June 13,1996). http://www.nytimes. com/library/cyber/ week0613decency.html

p. 78, par. 2–3, Ibid.

p. 78, par. 5–p. 79, par. 1, ACLU, "Victory!"

p. 79, par. 3, Ethical Spectacle Web site, "Senator Exon Press Conference After Philadelphia Ruling," http://www. spectacle.org.freespch/express.html

CHAPTER SIX

p. 80, par. 2, Horace Towner, *Our Highest Court* (Charlottesville: University of Virginia Library), 1994, http://etext.lib. virginia.edu/modeng/modengJ.browse.html, pp. 617–618.

p. 80, par. 3, Ibid.

p. 80, par. 4, Author's interview with Ann Beeson, May 31, 2005.

p. 82, par. 2, Ibid.

p. 82, par. 3, Marjorie Heins, *Not in Front of the Children:*

"Indecency, Censorship, and the Innocence of Youth. New York (Hill and Wang, 2001), pp. 174–175.

p. 82, par. 4, Author's interview with Chris Hansen, May 16, 2005.

p. 82, par. 6, Ibid.

p. 82, par. 7, Enough is Enough, et. al., Amici Curiae Brief, http://www.ciec.org/SC_appeal/970121_EIE_brief.html

p. 83, par. 2, Ibid.

p. 84, par. 1, Neil Lewis, "Walter Dellinger: In Defense of the Constitution," *Duke University Alumni Magazine*, http://www.dukemagazine.duke.edu/alumni/dm10/dellinger.html

p. 84, par. 2, Tony Mauro, "High Gloss(U.S. Solicitor General Seth Waxman)," *American Lawyer* (October 2000), p. 96.

p. 84, par. 2, Jonathan Groner, "Seth Waxman," *Legal Times*, July 19, 2004.

p. 84, par. 3, Department of Justice Brief (filed with the Supreme Court on January 21, 1997), http://www.swiss.ai.mit.edu/6805/articles/ cda/reno-v-aclu-appeal.html

p. 85, par. 3, Ibid.

p. 85, par. 5, Ibid.

p. 85, par. 6–p. 86, par. 4, ACLU Brief of Appellees: *Reno* v. *ACLU* 1, www.aclu.org/Privacy/Privacy/cfm?ID=13922&c=252

p. 86, par. 5–p. 87, par. 1, Pamela Mendels, "A Plaintiff's Journey in Search of Justice," *New York Times* (March 20, 1997), http://www.nytimes.com/library/cyber/week/032097decency-hauman.html

p. 87, par. 3–5, "How the Court Works," Supreme Court Historical Society, http://www.supremecourthistory.org

p. 87, par. 7, Supreme Court Trial Transcript, No. 96-5111 (*Reno* v. *ACLU*), http://archive.aclu.org/issues/cyber/trial/sctran.html

p. 87, par. 8–p. 88, par. 3, Ibid.

p. 88, par. 5–p. 89, par. 4, Ibid.

SUPREME COURT JUSTICES

p. 92, par. 2–5, "William Hubbs Rehnquist," Biography

Resource Center Online, Gale Group (1999), http://gale net.galegroup.com/servlet/BioRC

p. 93, par. 2, "(Supreme Court Justices) John Paul Stevens," Professor Michael Ariens, http://www.michaelariens.com/ ConLaw/justices/stevens.htm

p. 93, par. 3, "Stevens, John Paul" Biography Resource Center, Gale Research (1998), http://galenet.galegroup.com/ servlet/bioRC

p. 93, par. 6–7, "O'Connor, Sandra Day," *Encyclopedia of World Biography*, Farmington Hills, MI: Gale Research, 1998), http://galenet.galegroup.com/servlet/bioRC

p. 94, par. 2, "(Supreme Court Justices) Scalia, Antonin," Professor Michael Ariens, http://www.michaelariens.com/ ConLaw/justices/scalia.html

p. 94, par. 2, "Scalia, Antonin," *Encyclopedia of World Biography*, (Farmington Hills, MI: Gale Research, 1998), http:// galenet.galegroup.com/servlet/bioRC

p. 94, par. 3, "Scalia, Antonin," Professor Michael Ariens, op. cit.

p. 94, par. 6–p. 95, par. 1, "Kennedy, Anthony," *Encyclopedia of World Biography*, (Farmington Hills, MI: Gale Research, 1998), http://galenet.galegroup.com/servlet/bioRC

p. 95, par. 4, "Souter, David Hackett," *The Columbia Electronic Encyclopedia*, New York: Columbia University Press, 2005, http://www.infoplease.com/ce6/people/A0846021.html

p. 95, par. 5, "Souter, David Hackett," Biography Resource Center Online, Thomson Gale (2005), http://galenet.gale group.com/servlet/bioRC

p. 95, par. 8–p. 96, par. 1, "Thomas, Clarence," *Encyclopedia of World Biography* (Farmington Hills, MI: Gale Research 1998), http://galenet.galegroup.com/servlet/bioRC

p. 96, par. 4–p. 97, par. 1, "Ginsburg, Ruth Bader," *Encyclopedia of World Biography* (Farmington Hills, MI: Gale Research, 1998), http://galenet.galegroup.com/servlet/ bioRC

p. 97, par. 3, "Stephen G. Breyer," *Newsmakers* 1997, Issue 4 (Gale Research 1997), http://galenet.galegroup.com/ servlet /BioRC

p. 97, par. 4, "Breyer, Stephen" *Encyclopedia of World Biography* (Farmington Hills, MI: Gale Research, 1998), http://galenet.galegroup.com/servlet/BioRC

p. 97, par. 5, Breyer, *Newsmakers*.

CHAPTER SEVEN

p. 98, par. 2, John Schwartz and Joan Biskupic, "Supreme Court Rejects Curbs on Online Speech," *Washington Post* (June 27, 1997), p. A01.

p. 98, par. 4, Joshua Quittner, "Unshackling Net Speech: In its First Foray Into Cyberspace, the Supreme Court Says the First Amendment Applies There Too," *Time* (July 7, 1997), p. 28.

p. 98, par. 5–p. 100, par. 3, Supreme Court Opinion, No. 96-511, *Reno*. v. *ACLU*, http://www.ciec.org/SC_appeal/opinion.shtml

p. 100, par. 5, Concurrence by O'Connor/Rehnquist, No. 96-511, *Reno* v. *ACLU*, http://www.ciec.org/SC_appeal/concurrence. shtml

p. 101, par. 2, "Supreme Court Rules: Cyberspace Will Be Free! ACLU Hails Victory in Internet Censorship Challenge" (June 26, 1997), http://archive.aclu.org/news/n062697a.html

p. 101, par. 5, Author's interview with Ann Beeson, May 31, 2005.

p. 103, par. 2, Wendy Herumin, *Censorship on the Internet: From Filters to Freedom of Speech* (Berkeley Heights, NJ: Enslow Publishers, 2004), pp. 39–40.

p. 103, par. 4, "ACLU and Others Challenge Internet Censorship Bill Signed by President Clinton," http://www.aclu.org/Privacy/Privacy.cfm?ID=13753&c=252

p. 103, par. 5, Center for Democracy & Technology, "The Court Challenge to the Child Online Protection Act," http://www.cdt.org/ speech/copa/litigation.shtml

p. 104, par. 4, *Ashcroft* v. *Reno* Oral Arguments, Transcript, http://www.supremecourtus.gov/oral_arguments/argument_transcripts/03-218.pdf

p. 105, par. 2, Ibid.

p. 105, par. 4, Ibid.

INTERNET SAFETY ACTIVIST

p. 106, par. 6–p. 107, par. 2, Author's phone interview with Donna Rice Hughes, July 22, 2005.

p. 107, par. 4, Donna Rice Hughes with Pamela T. Campbell, *Kids Online: Protecting Your Children In Cyberspace* (Grand Rapids, MI: Fleming H. Revell, 1998).

p. 108, par. 1, Interview with Hughes, July 22, 2005.

p. 108, par. 4, Ibid.

p. 109, par. 1–2, *Ashcroft* v. *ACLU*, Opinion of the Court, http://www. supremecourtus.gov

p. 109, par. 4, Linda Greenhouse, "Court, 5-4, Blocks a Law Regulating Internet Access," *New York Times* (June 30, 2004).

p. 110, par. 4, Henry J. Kaiser Family Foundation, "See No Evil: How Internet Filters Affect the Search for Online Health Information," http://www.kff.org/entmedia/20021210a-index. cfm

p. 110, par. 5, *U.S.* v. *ALA*, Transcript, Oral Arguments, www.supremecourtus.gov

p. 111, par. 2, Ibid.

p. 111, par. 5, Ibid.

p. 111, par. 7, *U.S.* v. *ALA*, Opinion of the Court, http://www.supreme courtus.gov/opinions/02pdf/02-361.pdf

p. 113, par. 2, David Finkelhor, Kimberly J. Mitchell, and Janis Wolak, "Online Victimization: A Report on the Nation's Youth," Crimes Against Children Research Center, University of New Hampshire (2000), http://www.unh. edu/ccrc/

p. 113, par. 4–5, Kimberly J. Mitchell, David Finkelhor, and Janis Wolak. "The Exposure of Youth to Unwanted Sexual Material on the Internet: A National Survey of Risk, Impact, and Prevention," *Youth & Society* (March 2003).

FREE SPEECH ACTIVIST

pp. 114–115, Author's interview with Patricia Nell Warren, July 15, 2005; "Patricia Nell Warren," http://www.wildcatintl.com/partners/pbw.htm

p. 116, par. 2–3, Richard Jerome, "The Cyberporn Generation: As the First Kids to Grow Up with Internet Porn Come of Age," *People Weekly* (April 26, 2004), p. 72.

p. 116, par. 4–p.117, par. 1, Finkelhor, Mitchell, and Wolak. "Online Victimization."

p. 117, par. 2–3, Bob Meadows, "Researchers Look at How Online Porn Can Color a Child's View of Love and Sex," *People Weekly* (April 26, 2004), p. 72.

p. 117, par. 5–p. 118, par. 1, National Research Council, "Youth, Pornography, and the Internet," Executive Summary, http://www.nap.edu/books/0309082749/html

p. 118, par. 2, Author's interview with Donna Rice Hughes, July 22, 2005.

p. 118, par. 3, Finkelhor, Mitchell, and Wolak, "Online Victimization."

p. 118, par. 6, Ibid.

p. 119, par. 1, Author's Interview with Rheana Parrenas.

p. 119, par. 2, Finkelhor, Mitchell, and Wolak, "Online Victimization."

FurTHer inFormaTion

BOOKS

Allport, Alan. *Freedom of Speech*. Philadelphia: Chelsea House Publishers, 2003.

Farish, Lea. *The First Amendment: Freedom of Speech, Religion, and the Press*. Springfield, NJ: Enslow Publishers, 1998.

Friedman, Samuel Joshua. *Children and the World Wide Web: Tool or Trap?* Lanham, MD: University Press of America, 2000.

Henderson, Harry. *Issues in the Information Age*. San Diego, CA: Lucent Books, 1999.

Herumin, Wendy. *Censorship on the Internet: From Filters to Freedom of Speech*. Berkeley Heights, NJ: Enslow Publishers, 2004.

Jerome, Richard. "The Cyberporn Generation: As the First Kids to Grow Up with Internet Porn Come of Age, Researchers Look at How Online Porn Can Color a Child's View of Love and Sex," *People* magazine, April 26, 2004, p. 72.

Klinker, Philip A. *The First Amendment (The American Heritage History of the Bill of Rights)*. Englewood Cliffs, NJ: Silver Burdett Press, 1991.

Levert, Suzanne. *The Supreme Court*. New York: Benchmark Books, 2002.

Meadows, Bob. "The Web: The Bully's New Playground," *People*, March 14, 2005, p. 152.

Quittner, Joshua. "Unshackling Net Speech: In its First Foray Into Cyberspace, the Supreme Court Says the First Amendment Applies There Too," *Time*, July 7, 1997, p. 28.

Zeinert, Karen. *Free Speech—From Newspapers to Music Lyrics (Issues in Focus)*. Springfield, NJ: Enslow Publishers, 1995.

WEB SITES

American Civil Liberties Union
http://www.aclu.org

American Library Association
http://www.ala.org

Citizens Internet Empowerment Coalition
http://www.ciec.org

Crimes Against Children Research Center
http://www.unh.edu/ccrc/

Office of the Solicitor General
http://www.usdoj.gov/osg/

Oyez Project: U.S. Supreme Court Multimedia
http://www.oyez.org/oyez/frontpage

Protectkids.com
http://www.protectkids.com

Supreme Court of the United States
http://www.supremecourtus.gov

Supreme Court Historical Society
http://www.supremecourthistory.org

BIBLIOGRAPHY

BOOKS AND ARTICLES

Elmer-DeWitt, Philip. "On a Screen Near You: Cyberporn—It's Popular, Pervasive and Surprisingly Perverse, According to the First Survey of Online Erotica. And There's No Way to Stamp it Out." *Time* (July 3, 1995).

____. "Fire Storm on the Computer Nets: A New Study of Cyberporn, *(Time*, July 24, 1995), p. 57.

Finkelhor, David, Kimberly J. Mitchell, and Janis Wolak. "Online Victimization: A Report on the Nation's Youth," Crimes Against Children Research Center, University of New Hampshire (2000), http://www.unh.edu/ccrc/

Heins, Marjorie. *Not in Front of the Children: "Indecency," Censorship, and the Innocence of Youth.* New York: Hill and Wang, 2001.

Hentoff, Nat. *The First Freedom: The Tumultuous History of Free Speech in America.* New York: Delacorte Press, 1980.

Hoyt, Holga G., and Edwin P. Hoyt. *Censorship in America.* New York: The Seabury Press, 1970.

Kolbert, Kathryn, with Zak Mettger. *Censoring the Web (Justice Talking from NPR).* New York: The New Press, 2001.

Meadows, Bob. "The Web: The Bully's New Playground," *People,* March 14, 2005, p. 152.

Mendels, Pamela. "3 Judges. 3 Voices. 1 Conclusion." *New York Times* (June 13, 1996).

Mitchell, Kimberly J., David Finkelhor, and Janis Wolak. "The

Exposure of Youth to Unwanted Sexual Material on the Internet: A National Survey of Risk, Impact, and Prevention," *Youth & Society* (March 2003), http://www.unh.edu/ccrc/Youth_Internet_info_page.html

Quittner, Joshua. "Unshackling Net Speech: In its First Foray Into Cyberspace, the Supreme Court Says the First Amendment Applies There Too," *Time* (July 7, 1997), p. 28.

Wallace, Jonathan, and Mark Mangan. *Sex, Laws, and Cyberspace*. New York: Henry Holt, 1997.

Woodward, Bob, and Scott Armstrong. *The Brethren: Inside the Supreme Court*. New York: Simon & Schuster, 1979.

COURT DOCUMENTS

Butler v. *State of Michigan*, 352 U.S. 380 (1957).

Roth v. *U.S.*, 354 U.S. 476 (1957).

Jacobellis v. *Ohio*, 378 US 184 (1964).

Ginsberg v. *New York*, 390 U.S. 629 (1968).

Miller v. *California*, 412 U.S. 15 (1973).

FCC v. *Pacifica Foundation*, 438 U.S. 726 (1978).

Renton v. *Playtime Theatres*, 475 U.S. 41 (1986).

Sable Communications v. *FCC*, 492 U.S. 115 (1989).

Reno v. *ACLU*, 521 U.S. 844 (1997).

U.S. v. *American Library Association*, 539 U.S.194 (2003).

Ashcroft v. *ACLU*, 542 U.S. 656 (2004).

index

about the author

Joan Axelrod-Contrada is the author of several books for middle-school and high-school students. She has written about a variety of topics, including women leaders, the Lizzie Borden trial, colonial America, and soccer player Mia Hamm. She is currently at work on a new book for Marshall Cavendish about drug abuse and society. The author's work has also appeared in the *Boston Globe* and various other publications, including *Writer's Digest*. In addition, she teaches a freelance writing course at the University of Massachusetts in Amherst. She and her husband, Fred, a newspaper reporter, are the parents of two Internet-savvy teenagers, Amanda and Rio.